Becoming A Beacon

Observations from a Guy Working Through His Own Crap

2nd Edition

Rich Levesque

Rich Levesque

Copyright © 2018 by Richard Levesque

All rights reserved. No part of this book may be reproduced in any form or by any electronic or mechanical means including information storage and retrieval systems-except in the case of brief quotations embodied in critical articles or reviews-without permission in writing.

The book is sold with the understanding that the author or publisher is not engaged in rendering any professional service. If expert assistance is required, please seek the services of a qualified professional.

This book is not intended as a substitute for any medical advice. If medical advice or other expert help is needed the services of an appropriate professional should be sought.

All brand names and product names used in this book are trademarks, registered trademarks, or trade names of their respective holders. The author or publisher are not associated with any product or vendor in this book.

Dedication

To **Hannah And Andrew**,
May you seek your own paths on your
terms with no apologies.

Rich Levesque

"Nothing can dim the light that shines from within."
Maya Angelou

Contents

Prologue:
So, I Did a Thing...

I went way the hell out of my comfort zone this weekend. I treated myself to an early birthday gift when I booked a trip to Western Massachusetts and went to an Evolving Out Loud retreat hosted by one Kyle Cease. I found Kyle by accident one day going "down the rabbit hole" on YouTube about a year ago. I tripped over his "How Enlightened Families Argue" video (watch it, it is hysterical), and continued to binge on others. I watched other folks in the transformation field as well, but I found myself returning to his stuff; it seemed his messages were what I needed to hear in any particular moment. Longer offerings, such as "The Limitation Game" and "Deep Down" were eventually purchased as was his book *I Hope I Screw This Up* (pre-ordered two months before it came out, not my "modus operandi"). The funny thing is, he's not what I would consider an in-your-face marketer, but I just wanted more and was like "JUST SHUT UP AND TAKE MY MONEY!!!" I'm kind of cheap with treating myself, so that says something.

Kyle is very much on this same journey with you, as in his own word, "co-creator" instead of a know-it-all "guru" from up high. He nudges you along to find your own answers. He isn't out reinventing the wheel, but he presents it in a way that it sticks.

I pondered flying out to California for his event earlier this month, but that would have meant a cross country flight to a place I have never been with a lot of things going on. For me that's just a bit overwhelming.

I couldn't pass it up when I saw Kyle was coming to Massachusetts. This event was taking place at Kripalu, a yoga retreat center near the New York border in Stockbridge. Seemingly an awkward fit, as yoga is a complete stranger, but I registered anyway. Booked it, done.

Timing was perfect as I was in a very deep rut. I had been in a writing slump where creativity just stopped flowing. I was at a crossroads, trying to figure out what was next. Life situations were adding to the frustration and confusion, and I just felt lost.

I went into this wide open with hope that something would click. Regardless of result I was spending a weekend in an area I love listening to someone I enjoy, so it should still be a win.

The ride up was mostly nice. I've always been much more of a "scenic route" kind of guy, so I avoided the highway. Landing was about an hour later than expected but it was worth it.

Just before the first session started, I pondered (that damn negative voice) whether Kyle could crush it as I heard he did the previous weekend in California. Having such a powerful weekend with 1400 people the weekend before, going across the country with an audience that was maybe 10% of that might not seem too exciting. About a minute into the event starting it was clear how ridiculous that thought was. He was just full on energy, truly excited to be there and to work with us. It was so obvious that this was just his genuine self, enthusiastic about sharing his message and truly appreciating everyone coming out. 90

minutes after the session ended, he was still in the hall talking to people.

I slept like crap that night. The temperature in the dorm was about 90 degrees. It was also an adjustment sleeping in a room hearing snoring, tossing, and farting that wasn't your own. 5:30 am eventually came. Being a night person makes it a challenge to appreciate what a nice time of day it actually is. After a little meditation came breakfast in the cafeteria. I said hello to the attendant and the daggers staring back were a stern reminder that breakfast was silent, as in no talking. Oops. I must say though, it was such a grounding experience eating in silence with only your own thoughts. And clanging plates. And banging trays. Almost felt like a concert.

What an amazing Saturday it was, I learned a ton about myself going through the exercises and listening to others' stories. I had a lot working through me: where I am at, what I want and do not want, where did I desire to take life next.

When Saturday's second session ended, while talking to someone else, I found myself waiting in line to speak to Kyle. I was having conversations with others moving in and out and I realized I was 2 people away. My reaction was "How exactly did I get here?", but I just rolled with it. Let's face it, I wasn't exactly in a rush to be anywhere at the moment. About 45 minutes after the session ended Kyle Cease gives me a huge hug and says, "Hello Rich (we had name tags-nobody's THAT good!), thank you for being here." The expected quick thank you turned projectile vomiting my whole life story to him, then how I got into writing and my book idea. He listened intently and was very supportive. He says to me "The world needs your book to happen. I want you to promise me right now that you will have the first chapter done next Sunday. Then one chapter done every Sunday night until it's written. You promise?" Like a small child that was just offered ice cream I nodded. Then he gave me another hug and said, "Thank you for your words and I can't wait for your book." Holy. Shit. Blown. Away.

Sunday morning was just so peaceful. I found a pleasant empty corner for meditation and was ready for the last session. Which was more of the same from the previous two days really. It was a good thing. Holy crap, what a weekend.

Of course, I couldn't just drive straight home. I just needed to drive aimlessly for a while. I took the Mohawk Trail, which is this awesome yet very twisty and occasionally scary mountain road. Which gets even scarier when you start to fall asleep while driving it. Thankfully there was a place to pull over close by and I took a couple hour nap. After waking up and working through the trail I started having all these crazy ideas fly through me. I just kept driving. I still have so, so much to process but it was very much the dynamite needed to blow out some serious boulders. I'm in no rush but I'm just letting stuff flow as it is ready to do so.

Part of my post-event commitment is to write for a minimum of 30 minutes every morning for 90 days. That writing is where the meat of this book comes from. Don't worry, this book isn't going to be 90 long ass journal entries. Some were redundant, others felt too personal. A few were just better served to be presented in other places.

The book involves ideas that passed through as I wrote that felt right and true in the moment. Ideas relating to my own story and documenting my own growth. The belief is that most will resonate to you, the reader, in some way. There may be points that you will find yourself screaming out in your head "Right on!!!", and others may feel uncomfortable to address. Embrace all of that, because it is where you are in that moment. What I want is for readers to search in that deep-down place and see all these concepts through your own hearts, eyes, and experiences. I want you to work through these and come up with your own truth and answer to that. Initiate difficult conversations within ourselves and among others. Acknowledge and embrace where we align, and to respect and accept where we do not. "Not aligning" does not mean that the other person is wrong, only that their truth is different, no more and no less. Remember that.

What I seek for us to keep talking, seeking and growing while experiencing life in ways that align to ourselves rather than what we are "supposed" to be according to others. Just that alone will make the world a better place, because the searching and connecting that comes of it will lead to ideas flying out that people did not realize they had within. As ideas grow wings and fly, it will only lead to others creating their own as well. Even if an initially crappy idea can be a catalyst to something bigger, brighter, and more amazing. Let's start to fly.

Scene 1:
A Call to Souls

Once upon a time there was a guy. He entered middle age wondering why he was so depressed and miserable. Desperately hoping and believing there had to be more to life than what he was experiencing, which was a life and career that felt like a waste and a failure. This guy gave up multiple opportunities to follow his own path, so he could keep the acceptance of others and be stay where he didn't belong and settled into their expectations instead of his truth. This knowledge just ate him alive.

He viewed himself as an unlovable sellout making life choices based out of desperation, surrendering to a life that didn't call to him. He felt the need to hide from the world, apart from posting silly

Facebook memes, lame sports commentary, and spending time with people who just never really knew what he was all about. Granted some days, neither did he. The one absolute truth was that he knew that he wasn't wired for the world he was existing in.

I've plowed through and still am working through a lot of the same bullshit as most. The only possible difference is that I'm just becoming a little more aware of the specific stench of my shit. Still very much in the process of learning how to accept it, own it, and break free from it, I'm sharing my insights and experiences along the way, along with what gets stirred up through that process.

Please allow me through these pages to be your partner in crime, your wingman. Let's experience the highs, lows, and everything in between while trekking toward our individual journeys. Let's accept that there's a perpetual learning and growing process. We will continue to evolve for the duration of our time here and as we do, let's continue to be accountable to ourselves and each other. Let's feed off each other's energy by celebrating our successes and achievements, no matter the magnitude. Cheer each other on as we chip through our blockades and climb out of Elephant Shit Valley.

Let's take a deep breath, say "fuck it" and dive in. Obviously, I cannot force you to jump, but I can promise that once we get to the other side it WILL get so much better. So, why not?

I'm certainly not trying to convince anyone that "my way" is the only way, and I don't wish to shove any sort of "awakening" down anybody's throats. I wouldn't necessarily consider myself to be "awakened." People need to come strictly from their own free will, when they are open and ready to at least entertain the idea. All that said, if you're opening this book then I'm going to work off the assumption that you are at least willing to hear me out. I'm humbled and grateful for that alone.

I keep feeling called to create connections and opportunities for fostering unity, love. I also believe strongly that, while we come from different beliefs and experiences, we all ultimately want the same thing: to make our world a better place. Certainly, the majority of us, I think?

If each of us grows to find our true callings and embraces our gifts, each of us landing in our true spot in the jigsaw puzzle, the power generated by each of us would tilt the advantage the masses. It would send a giant message to our leaders that we know we can do it better, and back that shit up daily.

It would represent a paradigm shift; instead of following along like lemmings to whatever garbage we are force fed by media, society, our educational systems, and other suspects. Imagine what we could be capable of if we called out their bullshit for what it is? If we determined and followed our own truths rather than those dictated to us by CNN, Fox News, or MSNBC?

What can we accomplish if we challenged ourselves and each other to become our best? What if we empowered our children and grandchildren to do the same? Built each other up instead of looking for fault? Imagine every man, woman, and child grabbing the world by its gonads, engaging their true callings. Every single one of us, answering that call from the universe with the roar of a lion! With light, fire, passion, and love! Without settling! Without lashing out! Without fear, hate, anger, pain! Breaking chains, smashing through ceilings, glass or otherwise! Embracing and honoring our own power, our own spirit! The many, connected as one! The one, connected with the many! With NO FUCKS GIVEN!

It will be new and different. It will lead to good days, horrible days, and all kinds of days in between. Overall, it will be amazing, wonderful, and empowering! All unique, beautiful gems shining in their own individually perfect lights, combining with those of others to create the most incredible prism ever imagined.

Do I know how this all will exactly play itself out? Do I know how we all manage to get to that place? Not at all, but it's not all mine to create. We all have a hand in that. All of us, at our max at the same time? Oh, hell yeah! We'll find many paths and many answers.

I am not asking anyone to give up any core beliefs, families, religion, politics, loves, and passions, that will be needed more than ever. I am imploring you to give back our limitations, doubts, and fears. I am challenging you to toss in all the chips and go all in on YOU! This is our challenge, our call. Are you ready?

Why am I going down this road? Because everywhere I look I see emptiness and unfulfilled dreams. I sense fear, despair, pain and anguish which lend to inauthenticity, anger, hate, surrender, and denial. People who are not being seen or heard, feeling trapped in unwanted roles. If we pay attention to what is behind what people are saying, they are screaming out, unable to express needs articulately. That we are doing the best we can with how we are hardwired and falling into the same traps as our previous generations have, just plugging along like good little sheep because that's all we know.

We don't know ourselves, our power, or our capacity for love. We haven't even caught a sniff of what our true potential may be. We believe we're supposed to settle for some life short of the one we dreamed. WE DON'T YET KNOW THAT WE CAN FLY!

We all know of motivational speakers, life coaches, and spiritual guides out there, carrying powerful messages of true transformation, breaking through inner walls, finding true self, and all that good stuff. Many of them are phenomenal and have tremendous, dead-on messages and very loyal followings. But what really happens though? Yeah, we finish the books, turn off the videos, return from out retreats and seminars. And for a while we are a house of fire, trying to change what we can and trying to connect. What happens when life comes along and kicks us in the crotch? We realize that our dreams require money that our checking accounts lack. They take time to develop, which gets lost for many reasons. We may get stuck working extra, or the furnace breaks, or an issue pops up with one of the kids. We may not have much support to deal with the shit that flies at us. The obstacles loom larger, and we eventually take our dreams and chuck them. Maybe we keep reading and watching stuff, but the old wiring wins out and up goes the old white flag. We just accept the boulders and blocks for what they are.

And that our little pocket chisels won't quite cut it for the size of the job at hand.

We're taught that we are on our own to pull ourselves up by our "bootstraps", that we are pretty much on our own to figure out our shit. Regardless of how high the pile is or how bad it smells, or so we are taught. That bootstrap thing? Yeah, it is only true up to a certain point. Of course, we do the bulk of the hard work, but there MUST be some help along the way or else nothing can happen.

We all had to learn our skills, hone our crafts, right? We didn't pop out of the womb with all these knowledge bombs! We must be mentored, take classes, read books, watch videos, learn by doing, and so forth. Every piece of information, instruction, and wisdom came from someone else that either donated their time or offered us their services at a cost.

We may have needed to obtain certifications, licenses, create LLCs, 501C3s, and other mandated paperwork saying that we are legally able to practice our skills, right? We can't just get grab some crayons and draw them, they must be granted to us after we demonstrate we have earned them.

If you work out of an office, workshop, storefront, basement, your home, anywhere, the space had to be secured from someone. Did you build it on your own? Great, but again, you had to get the space from someone. You likely took out a loan or grant to create the money needed to start up? Safe to assume you don't have a money tree, that had to be provided by someone else. And people must consume your goods and services, or else you won't be offering them for very long. Good luck doing that all by yourself. Do you now see where I am going? Yes, you worked your ass off, and you should be commended for that. But "no man is an island", regardless of whether we believe we are. Everyone needs help from others to survive, all of us. Community, it's how this all works.

Scene 2:
Lone Wolf and Inner Child

I am having a bitch of a time starting this one because it comes from a raw and painful place. Vulnerability? Holy hell, the idea putting myself out there makes me vomit. What would people think? Who will disown me? Will I get fired? How will I pay for my rent? I can fit my comforter nicely in a cardboard box when I get kicked out of my apartment, right? Well, if I'm going to encourage it, I'd better walk the talk. Deep breaths Richard....

Yeah, there are times where I choose to be the lone wolf. However, these times are not a choice as often as my life would make it seem. I got somewhat called out recently by someone close, likely without any deliberate intent other than to crack a joke in the moment. "Antisocial (me) who just randomly does this crazy shit you wouldn't expect." And honestly, it bothered me. Not that it was said, or that it was out of line. What irked me the most was the truth behind it. I couldn't deny it was something that I needed to hear. If anything, I am grateful that it happened because it forced me to address this internally. To dig deep and understand why and how. And to work on it.

There is a difference to me between a "lone wolf" and being "antisocial." The "lone wolf" may need to do a lot on his own, a lot of processing, understanding, seeking out of his own truth. At the end of the day, however, that wolf returns to the pack. Should this not be an option he creates his own, he doesn't stay isolated at the risk of his own well-being.

Yes, I am very much an introverted being. I must lay low at times to recharge the batteries. "Me time" doesn't happen and I feel like I am lost in the forest without a phone (I would say a flashlight or map but let's face it, our smartphones have them). My well-being goes to hell in a handbasket. People ask if I need a Snickers. But once I get a few hours or even a full day to reset I'm good to go. Now there are times where it becomes days, or weeks and it becomes an unhealthy problem. I've felt compelled to retract and disappear often, despite the damage it causes and the anxiety it creates.

Now why would I want to do that even as I know it's a problem? Doesn't it defy logic? Of course, most of this stuff does. But that is what happens when your mental and emotional health goes to shit. Logic goes right out the window.

More often than not I have felt like I didn't deserve anyone in my life. I felt unworthy of being anything but alone, and people really didn't want me around anyway. Once it became obvious what a steaming pile of trash I truly was, they would just abandon me.

Just like how I knew no one wanted me when I was a kid, and I wasn't good enough for my parents or to play with at recess, except to be made fun of or beat up. That I wasn't good enough to be part of anything that was going on.

I grew into the kid that wanted to be left the hell alone. That desired to hide behind the stacks in his mom's bookstore for hours because he knew no one would find or bother him. It was always safer getting lost in the different worlds books offered than it ever was in his own world. Yeah, it was lonely. Of course, it would have been so much more fun being with my peers and causing all kinds of shenanigans. Ultimately though, solitude was so much better than being everybody's favorite punching bag. The inner and outer bruises could heal a little bit before the next attack. There was always a next attack.

In middle school and early into high school it just got worse. Written on. Stabbed with pens. Stuff destroyed in my locker. Glasses broken. Clothes ripped. Shoes tossed in a toilet and shit on. Thrown into trash barrels and dumpsters. Spit on. Food dumped on me. Having the whole cafeteria chanting stuff at me. Even the ones that were "friends" would eventually turn on me and join the pile on, as did almost every girl I grew any sort of crush on.

I would come home off of the bus and get chewed out for the condition I usually came back in. I never told my parents what was really going on, which didn't help but I'm not sure they would've known what to do if I did.

8th grade was probably the worst of it, and probably when I had my first significant round with depression. However, this was 30 years ago, and no one really grasped any of that stuff back then. I went from being an A student to Cs and Ds. I was always "sick" and went to school as little as possible. And when I did go I was in the nurse's office by 3rd period and I would somehow have willed myself to a 100-degree fever, which meant I had to go home. Honestly, part of me wishes that I still had that fever-spiking talent.

I couldn't do any homework, I just couldn't. Even when I would actually try. I was just in a fog and didn't care. I couldn't care. Book reports wouldn't get done, homework assignments weren't passed in. I couldn't do it. I had no idea why.

My parents were completely embarrassed by me. They kept having to get called into school. They constantly were on me for being a lazy teenager and kept harping on my being a disgrace. They threatened to send me to a boarding school or to give me up to social services. They took away anything and everything I had interest in-books, being outside. They told me I couldn't play baseball, couldn't watch the Red Sox on TV (baseball was one of the only things that snapped me out of the funk most days). They took away my music, everything. The more they punished me the worse it got.

All I knew was that I was broken and a failure, coping with it completely on my own at 13. I thought the best way out was to die. I didn't want to be broken anymore. My parents would be relieved of their embarrassment. At school all the teachers and students would celebrate. I would no longer be a problem to anyone. Win-win, right? One afternoon after school I grabbed a belt and went to go hang myself in my bedroom closet. I wasn't careful enough and my brother (who was about 8 at the time) caught me and begged me not to do it, bawling his eyes out. As shitty an older brother as I was to him, he still wanted me around. So, I put the belt away feeling even shittier, having done that to the poor kid. And I was still alive to deal with more torture the next day. I just sucked at everything.

Not too far after that debacle I got sick. Legitimately sick this time, with pneumonia. It was the best thing that could have happened. It forced me to just sit, between coughs, and get myself together. I still don't really know how it happened, but somehow it did. I kept getting work from school to do. I really enjoyed being able to study and teach myself. I found myself enjoying learning and flying through my homework. My grades skyrocketed while I was in bed. Having my parents nursing me back to health helped a lot. I didn't feel like I was as much of a monster. It seemed like things were back to normal, although I am not sure my lungs would agree.

Once I recovered from the pneumonia, and just as randomly as I plummeted in that dark place, I snapped right back out of it. Life sort of just went back to its default setting. Almost like 8th grade never really happened. My grades shot right back up. While socially life was still rough for another year and a half or so there was light and a little clarity.

That summer I took an acting class and I just fell in love with being on the stage. Up there I could be anything, I could feel anything. And it was perfect. It felt like my star shined when I performed. Like I owned the world when those bright lights came on. And through theater I started to find many of the pieces who grew to be my "tribe" through high school. I felt like I was a part of something amazing. I was not only a part of it, but I was a WANTED part of it.

I don't know why or how, it was just this road through this dark scary forest, and I somehow bumbled down this path that led me through a dark forest before eventually finding myself back into the sunlight.

They should make T shirts that say "I survived age 13" on them. Seriously. For kids AND parents. I should go back and talk about my parents for a second. Because part of that recollection made them appear as though they were monsters. In my 13-year-old mind they kind of were. However, I swear on everything that they weren't. You see, this was an uncharted, scary place for them. Their first child just snapped, becoming a virtual stranger to them. They lost connection with him completely and they couldn't figure out how to repair it or why this was happening. Something was wrong with their biggest love and their brightest joy (okay second, they did like my brother more), out of the blue he was gone. Their son wasn't their son anymore. Back in those days there wasn't exactly much in the way of help available for them. It also didn't help much that, especially back then, their own internal wiring didn't allow for them to reach out. Remember, 30 years ago nobody really knew what depression was, and if they did they certainly never discussed it openly. Today it would have been identified easily and I would have been in some form of treatment. Back then, I was labeled as a "problem child."

They felt the world calling them failures as parents. It was bad enough that the school was starting to question them regularly. Imagine what other crap would come their way if people kept catching wind of what was occurring with me? How harshly would their friends, or their fellow churchgoers, judge them? They were convinced that my grandparents would; as most of their own childhood stories involved their constantly receiving the message that they weren't enough. So that to fire up all kinds of triggers in both. They had nothing to fall back on than to double down on what they knew from their experience. And this encouraged rendering tough love with the hopes that it would give me the kick in the ass that was needed. It was about as successful as the movie Gigli.

Running out of ideas and just throwing shit against the walls led to threats of sending me away. Going back with a more realistic eye, that NEVER would have happened. Those threats were the equivalent of throwing a desperate Hail Mary pass, because they WERE desperate and scared. They just wanted their kid back and went with what they knew, without anything in the way of help and guidance. They did their best. They loved me tremendously. Please see it from their eyes, because now as an adult I can, and I can still feel their anguish and desperation.

I feel so grateful now that I was able to come back to this. I really felt like for the first time I was able to sit with that 13-year-old and let him know that he wasn't broken after all. That he just in some tough space. Life did eventually get better for him. Younger Rich really was loved, but at the time no one knew what to do to help him. He always had something to offer to the world, even if not everyone could see it. I wish I had known to do that when I was 13, maybe I would've avoided some of the other traps I fell into through ensuing years.

High school ended up being a much better experience, even if was a roller coaster type experience. Toward the end my parents separated, with my dad leaving permanently on graduation day. As hard as that whole experience was in the moment, I thankfully had a lot of amazing support. I went away to college after, for no other reason than to meet the expectations of others. As with most endeavors you really aren't feeling, so went college. Certainly, from an academic standpoint. I just floated at first, then floating turned into falling. Regardless, I still managed to find my "tribes" there as well. I was blessed to be able to find these "families" at certain important points in my life.

Good news, I always found tribes. Bad news, they never lasted very long. Every time I found a tribe I found myself pushing them away, returning to that life as the Lone Wolf. Festering in my emotional blockages, I felt compelled to isolate myself from the world. Keeping myself hidden even though I was screaming out to be loved and included.

As I got older this urge only intensified. Any time I got close with anyone and any group of people it just became inevitable that my self-destruct mechanism would activate. I would either walk away or behave so ridiculously that it would force the issue. I never really understood why. I always convinced myself I was being abandoned again. Upon reflection, the blame usually lay at the feet of the guy in the mirror. I was almost always the one that initiated the separation sequence, as though I was fulfilling my role in the prophecy. I unconsciously deemed this necessary for dealing with what was inevitable on my own terms apparently.

Even when I don't run, it's at the core of so much of my shitty self-talk. While I at least THINK I am better at catching it, and I am, it's still quite rough at times. I still expect to get piled on, called out in the end so if I initiate it before anyone else can I can neutralize the attack before it starts. That's pretty fucked up if you think about it.

I found the lone wolf life, or the lone wolf life found me. Either works. I accepted that this was how it always had to be. And this kept me somewhat distant, even when I didn't want to be. However, something always gnawed from the inside. Chewed at me fierce, like a relentless bear. What I never realized was that it was that scared, broken kid. He still felt misunderstood and unheard, unable to comprehend the safety that truly existed around him. He always kept screaming out, begging for me to restrain myself. He has always sat in expectation of the "other shoe" to drop, to find out that everything was all just a crock of shit. That one day I would walk into a room and everyone would just start laughing at me, throwing crap at me, tossing me into another dumpster.

Of course I realize this sounds fucking ridiculous, but when there's a "broken" 13-year-old inside who only knows feeling unloved and unwanted? To that kid, this garbage is his truth and his reality. To him, that idea is anything but ridiculous. He is so desperate for love, belonging, and acceptance but he is also so locked into his defense mechanisms. He must be ready for it to all come apart because that is all he knows. He doesn't know what unconditional love is, or what to do with it.

He needs to push people away as a preemptive strike to protect himself from what he has been wired to believe comes next. He sees himself as inevitably a giant embarrassment to those around him, a source of shame to his family. He has no idea just how intelligent he truly is, or how gifted, kind, and passionate he is. He doesn't grasp the depth of his soul or the power he possesses. He doesn't see that his parents really did love him very much while themselves trapped by their own hurting inner children. That they were doing the best they could, but they were just scared kids too.

He doesn't know that he was never ever broken, that everything landed as it was supposed to, that he was   doing the best he could with what he had at the time. He is unaware he was not only enough. More than just enough, he was a damn survivor. He is starting to see it now, slowly beginning to understand. He is listening and processing it all in his 13-year-old soul, and gradually putting the pieces together. This doesn't happen overnight, not such a giant sea change as this is. It happens in fits and starts, with ups and downs. There are growing pains. With days where it feels like things are going backward instead of forward.

But there is a difference these days as I simultaneously learn to understand it myself AND continue to support and teach that kid. I'm learning that I must stay in the room and work this out. Understanding that those in my life today and those that come along in the future had zero to do with the bullshit that happened when I was a kid. And that anything that does happen from here on out has absolutely zero to do with my past demons. Additionally, comprehending that most of what happened to me had zero to do with me at all. It has everything to do with where they are in life and with their perception of it. What I am in their world is their own creation based on their own eyes, ears, and souls. And how they react to me is theirs and theirs alone. With that important knowledge, I can just be. The rest is out of my control and has no effect on who I am.

If I do let it affect my being, that is a choice that I have chosen to make, and I am responsible for any repercussions. Some days are of course better than others, but I am learning. I would like to think that I am headed in the right direction.

Returning to those in the past, I'm learning to let that go. Forgiving all of it. Realizing that these were all kids too, and not monsters. Kids who were very likely going through their own pain and confusion; life at 13 is rough enough with what occurs naturally. Kids fall into their socially assigned pecking orders and do what they were wired to do. It was never personal. It was their perception that told them I was an outcast and unworthy, not anything I ever did or said. They were growing through shit too and didn't have the guidance there to process it different. It just was.

With that understanding I am discovering how to release that shit. To move on and to be more aware. To try to work on my end to show that kids need to be learned different wiring, different systems of being. The responsibility for that falls on everybody to do their part as they gradually learn to do so themselves. My job in the moment is to share what I am learning. In time, over months, years, and generations we will evolve. There will be less broken kids with shitty wiring. This will happen, and we will all be better for that. Part of my responsibility is to continue maintaining proper perceptions, and to continue being support to that kid, and to keep sharing that experience to help others do the same.

The short version is this, "antisocial" is no longer an option. Recharge as needed, then back out there you go. I'm loved, wanted, and needed. I'm more than enough. And I got work to do keeping shit like the above on repeat rather than some of the corkers my mind will generate when left to its own devices.

Scene 3:
Hey, It's My Birthday!

The calendar, as well as Facebook, say it's my birthday. My birth certificate tells me that I am now 43 years old. I liked age 42 better, for no other reason than it's "the answer to life, the universe, everything. (If you didn't get this, stop. Put this book down-temporarily-and start reading Hitchhiker's Guide to the Galaxy by Douglas Adams. Do it now. You can thank me by coming back to this book after.)

What also needs mentioning is that the number 42 is the uniform number of one of my heroes, Jackie Robinson. The number 43? Meh. What goes with 43? What do you automatically think of when you think 43? What am I missing? Okay, it was Richard Petty's car number, but I just can't get into racing that much. Sorry

NASCAR fans. In the moment 43 could be 26, 53, 63, 271, whatever. It's just a number. How you feel is really all that matters. Some days my body feels 73; I am working on that. Occasionally my maturity level is about 12. I don't really work on that all that much-it's part of my charm. Now my soul...forever 23? I can dig that.

For most of my life I viewed my birthday as a referendum on my status as an acceptable human being. I placed much of my value as a human on whether a cake or cards appeared, or if I got a call or a message from a certain person. This was never much of an issue as a kid, because of course I was spoiled on my birthdays then. The parental units were always amazing at pulling off the birthday stuff, regardless of whatever else was happening. That day I was always given the king treatment.

My 17th birthday was probably my first dose of "adult reality". Granted most of this was my own fault. I had pushed back writing my senior essay, you remember the one they made you send in with all your college applications? Yeah, that. It had to be turned in the next day and of course I hadn't finished it...or started it. Anxiety was very prevalent when it came to me and writing back in the day. Anxiety doesn't cut it, writing TERRIFIED me. I would stare at a blank page for days. More often than not (at least in high school) I would eventually work through it, only to have my work criticized. I heard such golden nuggets such as, "don't even bother taking the AP Exams because your writing is so bad you can't possibly pass" kind of suck (and yet I'm the one that's writing a book, so go figure). The thing was...I had all the necessary points but that I wrote like I talked, which I guess is bad? I never really did understand what exactly the problem was, I just let it create more anxiety when I wrote instead. Which of course was the healthiest possible solution (Before I continue, those AP exams? The first one was U.S. History my junior year. I listened to them and did not take the test. My senior year, for European History I took the attitude of, "Screw you, I'm taking this thing anyway!" I passed. Boom! I just needed to get that across. Moving on...).

Parked in front of the typewriter (remember those?), typing away. That's how I spent most of my day. Writing up some quality bullshit about my curiosity. Oddly that would more likely be truer now than it was then. Maybe the admissions people were blown away, maybe they didn't even read it, but either way I was accepted to every college I applied to. Granted I didn't apply to Harvard, but a win is a win, right?

Now getting back to Birthday 17, that day got gradually worse. I got a nasty call from my employer at the time, yelling at me about some paperwork or something (I may or may not have forgotten to have a new child labor permit drawn up at school or something). The woman did apologize the next day, but it felt like a pile on at the time.

College birthdays? They were a blast (what I can remember). Most of those stories don't necessarily need to be laid out in black and white. Use your imaginations! I had some awesome friends in college and we'll leave it at that.

After college, reality by way of adulthood set in. Of course, there were and are more important things we as adults need to focus on than birthdays, but for a long time I lacked interest in grasping that. I grew increasingly devastated year after year because of the lack of acknowledgement, and I reached a point where birthdays became dreaded because they presented another reminder, courtesy of my monkey mind, of how little I mattered to anybody.

Occasional years would bring pleasant surprises, but the majority of birthdays brought crickets. Expectations were set super low as I prepared myself for the worst. Always easier to start there and work up, right?

Working through this transformation thing the last couple of years, I've had a little bit of a birthday epiphany. It was a bit of tough love that played out something like this: "You spoiled brat, no one has any obligation to you. No one owes you anything. You want to enjoy your birthday? YOU go and do it yourself! Take care of yourself. Treat yourself. Most of all, LOVE YOURSELF! Let anything else just be a welcome bonus!"

Ding, ding, ding.... light bulbs, sirens, fireworks, you get the idea.

So, with that bomb of knowledge in pocket, the last couple of birthdays have been sweet. Last year I treated myself to an iPhone and bought myself a nice dinner from my favorite restaurant. This year I rewarded myself early by booking that retreat. Today I'll probably hit the open road and check out a bookstore or two, and maybe do something else I enjoy. Nobody else has any responsibility to coddle my ass, that lies on me. Don't misunderstand, that doesn't mean I'm not grateful to anyone who chooses to take a minute from their busy day to call me or send me a message. I most certainly am appreciative of any effort.

Revisiting all of this, I don't think that it ever dawned on me why I felt the way I did until I scribbled this out. When I was younger, it was the one day I was celebrated for being me, and for at least one day I didn't have to feel "not good enough". Once that went away it was crushing to me because I lost the one thing, the one time I would feel accepted, loved, wanted. When that was gone, my inner child was demoralized, and, in that heartbreak, I learned to accept this was reality. Hey, it's easier to handle if you know it's coming right? God, I believed in some galaxy class bullshit.

Thankfully what I am realizing these days is that birthday celebrations, like everything else, start with me. First and foremost, they need to begin from a place of self-love. Having learned this, I know it's my job to ensure that my inner child is loved and respected and feels safe and special. I get that now. And it is damn phenomenal to possess this knowledge. Enough writing, it's playtime. It IS my birthday, right?

Happy birthday Rich!
Love,
Rich

Scene 4:
Riding Out the Dark Voices

Recently I was watching someone I know on a Facebook Live. He spoke from a dark yet familiar place. A dank ravine filled with despair. When trapped in those depths, it felt foreign to believe one was anything other than a failure.

Many were listening and attempting to talk him down from his despondent perception. Unfortunately, he was just unable to process any of the love offered in his direction that day. Sometimes it can be so black that it is impossible to receive love, and this was his space on that day.

Too many instances to count, I have experienced that place where that asshole monkey parked in your brain is having itself a field day, loading up piles of its own shit and senselessly throwing it everywhere. The shit onslaught leaves your emotions as a steaming trash pile. A barrage stemming from the monkey ripping out each perceived flaw and failure and just rubbing your face into it. You drop so low after all of that self-assault that you have no energy left to exist, never mind to experience the beauty of life.

God, that is such a miserable place to reside. I really could empathize with what that poor guy was stuck in. Like, deeply feeling because I truly understand how dark of a place it all is.

Fortunately, in the last year or so I have been blessed to have learned a few tools to be able to recover quickly when the black days and dark nights of the soul resurface. I am grateful I know myself well enough to usually anticipate their arrival. I've observed when I experience a combination of extended heavy human interaction and a lack of sleep I am primed to have one of those days happen. With that knowledge I am rarely taken off guard when my moods go south.

I attempt to plan so I have few obligations scheduled when I am in danger of having an episode. I'll try to take a day off from work because I know I can become a liability when I go dark.

The initial attack comes over me like a giant tidal wave of monkey shit. I simply let the whole wave roll, resisting the urge to fight it. It gets to just do its thing and move on through. All the insults, every single "you suck", "you're not good enough", "why do you even bother", "nobody cares what you think", "these people really hate you," on and on.

I give all the emotions space to flow too. I don't fight them, merely observing them. I let them be felt. I let them do what they need to do, get sad, cry, or scream out in anger. I'll sit in all that pain and just stay out of the way.

If I absolutely must release anything it is in the form of writing, drawing, or through some creative space. The one thing off the table is interacting with people as it flows through. As much as it is counteractive to what we are taught, it is necessary for my process. Otherwise I end up latching on to some of the monkey's crap, becoming defensive, and attacking in some dickish, passive-aggressive sort of way. Believing the monkey when it tells me that people really aren't in your corner leads me to buy that the logical next step is to call them out on that. Thing is, 99% of the time the image the monkey is throwing at me is shit, with no truth to it at all. I'm just going to confuse and hurt innocent victims and by then the damage is done. Even if they did hurt me, I'm in no condition to go down that road therefore the phone stays off. No texting, no calling, no social media. Maybe I'll check every few hours in case there is any emergency but other than that nothing gets returned until I clear all of this.

When the wave rolls on, I remind myself that crap was nothing but thoughts, useless space takers. A few do try establishing a more permanent internal residence. Regardless of how believable they seem, dark thoughts are actually quite simple to debunk. I take these statements and question them. Ask for proof about why they are true. Lots of "How?", "Why?", and "Show your work please." Really grill them like your favorite TV detective going to town on a suspect. I have always found that one of two things will happen. These seemingly dark accusations either contradict themselves, or the monkey will be unable to provide any substantial proof. Inevitably, it will just slip off and disappear like a cat that broke an expensive vase. I'll keep repeating this process until I can clear what is necessary to get back into normal working order.

When the interrogations are complete, it's self-care time. Self-care to me usually means listening to a LOT of music. I'll really get into it for a while, letting the melodies and the lyrics serve as an internal scrub brush, cleaning out any leftover shit stains. Once I have worked my way through then I am good to go. I'll reconnect where I need to and proceed along my merry way.

Learning how to do this has been such an absolute godsend for me. What used to take weeks or months to fight through (if I even could do that) now takes at the most about 24 hours. The biggest thing is that I no longer fight it anymore; it just emboldens the crap.

The short version:
1. Learn when to expect when it'll happen. Your body knows. Listen and plan accordingly.
2. Disconnect from the oncoming emotional storm.
3. Don't fight it, ride it out without taking ownership of it. Just observe what you feel.
4. Investigate the leftover stubborn thoughts until they eventually prove fraudulent.
5. Clean out the soul with what reignites it.

I hope you'll learn as I did, that the crap has no permanent space allowed for it inside of you anymore. Anything that does come through is temporary at best and unwelcome for any extended stay. Exerting less energy fighting that garbage awards you more space to explore your gifts and goals, allowing you to tune into your soul and listen to what it has to say. The more you connect the more you begin to appreciate and, dare I say it, LOVE YOURSELF. There is nothing more freeing to the soul than locking onto what truly is, and that is love.

This is what worked for me, much better than anything else assigned to address my depression and anxiety. Learning how to manage my operation system allows me to maximize my growth. It feels quite amazing.

I hope that the guy I was listening to that day comes across this and encounters the same solace as I did.

Scene 5:
Owning Our Crap, Leaving Theirs

How the fuck does one learn how to tune out toxicity? I keep trying and keep failing hard, fast, and spectacularly, causing myself repeated aggravation. I know the answer is to work to avoid those situations but that can be impossible. I did finally have a recent watershed moment, as I kept running smack into these following reminders:

1. One's opinions of you are simply a representation of who THEY are. Nothing more, nothing less.

2. How you react to those opinions is as much of a representation of who YOU are. You cannot control the opinions of others, but you can have COMPLETE control over how you respond.

I have certainly added my share to assorted toxic environments over the years. I am by no means a victim, in spite of considering myself otherwise on multiple occasions. My perception of "justice" ignites my fiery reactions upon observing something that feels "wrong". I can't just roll my eyes or, heaven forbid, not respond. For whatever reason I feel compelled at times to preach my unwanted opinion from the mountaintops and then continue to obsess over the crap. This process has done absolutely nothing to foster growth or solutions, as could be expected. The problem is while in the moment I am usually too busy with being pissed off to care.

There was a potential "a-ha" moment recently. There is one person I know who continually must "stir the pot", can't help but drop a "so-and-so just said this about you, can you believe it?" I really don't suspect any of this is done with ill intent, but rather from a desire to fit in with the crowd, whoever is part of that crowd at the moment. I could be wrong, but I see nothing to indicate otherwise.

Now here's the thing, approximately 99.979999% I listen to it, take the bait, lose my shit, and flip out about it to anyone in a 50-yard radius. Which of course does nothing to alleviate what may already be an edgy situation, plus it draws people in that would much rather be left the fuck alone. Most of all, it doesn't align with any version of what I want for myself.

This last time, I chose not to partake. Well, somewhat. This party felt as though it was important that I be made aware of some crap that was being said about me. This time I said flat out, "I don't need to know, thank you." Through multiple attempts, I kept repeating my lack of interest in this knowledge. upon giving up, an attempt was made to turn the conversation to gossip about someone else. My response: "Look, if it's not spoken to me directly, it's not my business. Especially if it was told to you in confidence." That ended the conversation.

I managed to step up somewhat in that moment. Despite my improvement I was still kind of irritated about this whole interaction. Why? I remembered what someone much wiser than me said, when you're being fed all kinds of dirt about someone else, it is almost certain that the same person is feeding others dirt about you when you aren't around. Knowing that was the likely scenario kept pissing me off. I wish it didn't, but the truth is the truth.

The next day it was still there and as I meditated on it things did become clearer. I realized that this wasn't ever about my confidence being violated or me being involved with the same at another's expense. It all comes back to the one person who I am responsible for, and how that person handled everything. Me. I was the one that chose to look back. I was the one who kept taking the bait. I was the one who kept responding and taking pointless bullshit personally. This was solely on me! It's not my problem that people talk shit. It's not my problem people gossip. It's not my damn problem. It is not mine to own, not mine to accept. Why do I continue to treat this crap like it is?

What is the correct response by the way? It doesn't quite fit into our shitty wiring or our "automatic pilot" but this is the correct answer. You let them. That's right. Let them beat you up, call you names, gossip, lie. Let them do whatever the hell they want.

None of this is ever in our control. We can never make someone feel the way they want to about us. We can't force someone to support us. As the saying goes, "haters gonna hate". At the end of the day it has everything to do with their own perception and issues, and precisely zero to do with ours. Keep doing you, stay positive in your truth. Be the person you strive for before, during, AND after you leave the situation. Choose to be the person that operates from a place of love, not of revenge or self-protection. Those come from the egoic monkey mind. Stay in the positive and keep giving good juju into the universe. Rise above. You might even change a few hearts in the process. Whether your truth is accepted by others

or not isn't your worry, it never was. Your
growth is, so always rise above.

Scene 6:
Taking the Bait

I just worked an overnight shift for the first time in quite a while. I don't rebound from them the way I used to, which is sad considering I worked straight overnights for years back in the day. I enjoy them because when you get a call, you are truly needed. There isn't the drama and bullshit that you often get when most people are awake. The calls where your first instinct is to tell the person at the other end to grow the fuck up and figure it out like an adult. I've learned the hard way that dealing with the internal affairs investigation afterwards is just not worth that flash of satisfaction you get in the moment.

These days I normally work when the masses are still awake, and I often experience what most of us who deal with the public encounter day in and day out. How much of the shit that comes in is really about me? Almost none. As I figure things out I do find that is becoming easier to let the stupid shit roll off.

I start to see and comprehend that people are the way they are for reasons that I'll never know about. I don't have access to their experiences or their stories. Everyone has a story and it is not for anyone else to know unless it is offered. What needs understanding regardless is that the incoming garbage is simply how they are perceiving and then expressing their own situation through the pain and fear they are experiencing at that moment. Even when they are screaming at me and calling me a useless fucking asshole. It has nothing to do with me. (Give me a second, as I feel like I need to repeat this to myself in the mirror about 163,926 more times.)

I have a long path of damage and destruction behind me over my years because I never did fully comprehend that. My responses often created escalation and were inevitably followed by disaster. Almost every time I have gotten myself into a puddle of shit, it's been a result of my being provoked, taking the bait and devouring it like a rabid dog. It was me going automatically into "fight or flight" and right back at whoever initiated, often with twice the fury as what came in at me.

The first coherent thought comes seconds after I am already well into engagement and blown past the point of no return. Instead of attempting to diffuse the situation, the conscious process focuses on attempting to justify my actions.

This goes back to something I was taught by my dad and others, that many of us learn. The adage goes something like, "Do not ever throw the first punch. But if the other guy does, you then go to town and fuck him up."

I have gone down this road many times. Not so much physically, thankfully as I'm not a very big guy, but verbally? My mouth can run with the best of them, like the Energizer bunny. It didn't take very long to recall my accomplishments with that because it never really did a whole lot of anything. I may have been right, and the insults and one-liners might have been on point, but my prize at the end of the day was never a cookie, just a popsicle headache. I was the one called in to explain my actions, the one that got the target on his back. Even if I was 100% "in the right" it never mattered.

It's like in hockey where the ice officials never see the annoying defenseman insulting your mother and poking his stick into your ribs. They ALWAYS see the retaliatory sucker punch, and the guy that snaps is always the one sent to the penalty box, that's just how it ends up going down. The penalty incurred can end up screwing a team over far more than that opposing knucklehead defenseman ever could. Yeah, the first guy was being a dick, but all retaliation leads to is two dicks instead of one. Nothing was avenged or resolved, just a larger pile of crap needing to be maneuvered around. Congratulations.

So how do you stop yourself from instantly firing back? Or even firing back at all? Yeah, that's quite a challenge. In the heat of the moment you're just not going to be able to process alternative choices, different de-escalation methods, how to take it all for what it is and continue to be of assistance. "Fight or flight" is kicking in, but you can process this: breathe in, breathe out. Just keep taking deep breaths as you need to get to diffuse your own anxiety, to pull back your inner need to defend and attack. If you need to count or recite fact lists to help regain your focus, go for it, it may help. If not, just focus on your breathing.

While you're working through this process, the other person may continue to unleash at you, that's fine. It will probably make it even easier to resolve and redirect when you're ready. They'll be tiring, and it will make it easier for cooler heads to prevail. Just keep focusing on that breathing. What may feel like an eternity won't make or break a situation.

Remember, the shit flying in at you may be painful and uncomfortable, and will likely piss you off, but IT IS NOT ABOUT YOU! Don't lose track of this. Focus on keeping your own shit in control. Once you're back in check then you can focus on solving the issue at hand. Ask questions, explain the process and what you are doing to try and assist the other person in that moment. This often works to refocus the other person, and most of the time you should be good to go.

On occasion you'll come across someone you just can't diffuse. All you can do is keep doing the breathwork as needed and handle the situation as well as possible. Focus on removing yourself from the situation entirely, especially if a resolution is not going to be allowed. Send it up the chain of command if needed, let management making the bigger bucks bungle it up. Or if you have the option, walk away.

All in all, it's another work in progress. I'm still far from perfect but I am getting A LOT better. I still have some triggers that I keep digging through, and those will come as I keep doing the work. I am now discovering that in most of my day-to day-situations I am a lot less stressed and anxious, which indicates my well-being is in a much better place.

Okay now kids, continue to remember my three step Angry Aggressive Asshole Disengagement System:

1. Breathe, a lot
2. Focus on the task at hand (or at the very least anything other than how much you want to punch this asshole in the face)
3. Remove yourself if necessary

It will save you so much stress and hassle in life. You get enough challenges without creating new unnecessary ones.

Scene 7:
Dodging Pigeons

I was watching a video of a sweet young lady talking about taking people's shit personally. Particularly ringing true with me was the idea of being so locked into the garbage we lose track of ourselves. We piss away so much time and energy emotionally involved in this bullshit where it could be better used to create something amazing or even just enjoy this moment.

Think about all the times you've been criticized, called out, and rejected. Just sit and reconnect with all the comments, insults, and gestures. While you're in there, ask yourself how much of what was said or done TRULY about you? Be honest, don't let any emotions drive your answer. How much was really based on either the other person's state of mind or expectations? I'll bet you a coffee right now at least 90% of it falls into either one.

Give it a couple of minutes and then release it. Whatever way this works for you, just do it. Figure out how to let that shit fly away. Is it gone? You good? Great, then let's continue.

Yeah, you may be the target with the bright red bullseye, but it doesn't have anything to do with you. Just go on with your day. Don't waste time or effort on any of that.

Think of it like when a pigeon shits all over your car. Pigeon in the air doing pigeon things, thinking pigeon thoughts, going about its pigeon day. Pigeon has no clue or care or that it just carpet bombed a vehicle period, never mind who the car belongs to. Pigeon is long gone on its merry pigeon way by the time you get to see pigeon's nasty multicolored breakfast mess splattered all over your windshield. Pigeon has no awareness you're flipping out. Pigeon is across the city chowing down on lunch, which will soon explode all over the hood of some poor unsuspecting SUV in the wrong place at the wrong time. Pigeon isn't hosing your car off. Pigeon doesn't even realize there is anything to clean, or what cleaning is.

We just take a deep breath and grab the hose or seek out the closet car wash. Blast that shit off and go on. This is really what that 90% is, all pigeons shitting on you. Just clean it and roll on. It just is.

How about that other 10%? Well, we are human, with all the failings of humanity. Sometimes we just fuck stuff up, all we can do is accept and own our shit when the moment comes. Apologize as needed, make amends where you can, and move on. Learn the appropriate lesson and accept we cannot control the aggrieved parties' reactions. What's done is done, move the hell on. Harping on this any further only hurts us. Picking up a theme here about just letting it go and moving on? Good, that means you're paying attention. Go get a cookie.

This is a huge rewiring project. Some wires are fairly easy to swap out, yet there are many others that involve awkward, uncomfortable, and sometimes painful gymnastics to successfully reach. Bunches of wires that are a tangled hot mess, taking a lot of effort and patience. They can make you crank out curse words you never realized you knew. Eventually, after a lot of sweat and tears, they can come undone. Stick with it, keep falling and getting back up, as much as needed, over and over. You'll realize in time that you are falling just a little bit less, as with anything that you practice. Gradual improvements become more obvious to you. Awareness of more tangible points where you didn't let the crap suck you in, and you were able to let shit go. These moments should excite you just a little bit. Allow them to energize you as you continue to improve.

While working through this process, do you see yourself spending less time on others' bullshit? Where is that new found time and energy being used? Hopefully it's giving yourself permission to create, seek, learn, and share love and peace. Try to check in with yourself at least every week (and maybe more often as you feel the need but for this exercise a little longer duration helps with seeing distinct differences). Quickly go to a situation where you find yourself on the receiving end of crap that isn't yours. Do you find that you are handling it better? In what ways? If you can let go are you finding that you now have excess time and energy to give? Where is all of that being spent? How does that help you in your journey? Now check back in and see if there is something that was part of the small amount you are responsible for. What does the reparation process look like to you (apologies, making amends, etc.)? What kind of feedback did you receive after you owned your shit? How did it affect you? Were you able to let things go? Why or why not? If there were hang-ups what were they? How do you expect they will improve or even disappear going forward? Going through this checklist, be sure that while finding areas to work on that you are first and foremost giving yourself credit for every stride you make.

Remember that this shit doesn't turn on a dime. It's tough stuff. I still blow it far more than I care to admit. Inevitably someone gets you in the wrong mental and emotional space on the wrong day, and it likely will not end well. Such is life, don't kick yourself over it. Let it go and start over. The next crack will be better, or the one after that. This is changing out an entire way of living and installing a different one. It will come, you'll get this. It'll just take time.

Scene 8:
Sticking It

The word "commitment" has been floating in my head the last few days. Commitment is a concept which I have struggled with as long as I can remember. Funny how 90-day challenges tend to bring that shit to the forefront. Being well off the retreat high now, it's a lot harder for me to keep up. I am still staying in it though, which in itself is quite an accomplishment. This might be one small step in the big scheme, but it is still a plus for a guy with a shitty track record at holding to commitments. How many times have I intended to quit smoking, change my diet, stick to an exercise plan? I feel like I am the poster child for unfinished projects. Shit, that's a whole other book just listing those!

Admittedly much stems from being a kid and wanting to do things, but never being allowed to at all. Looking back, I know it had everything to do with the parental units fearing some horrific doom befalling me while I was out of their sight. Certainly, there was no bad intent, just an enduring irrational fear that their internal wiring taught them. Regardless, it can be quite rough to be a kid always hearing "no." Eventually I just stopped asking to do things or go places, I always knew the answer, so I gave up.

There was some improvement when I got my driver's license, but even that was by accident. My parents were so sure I would fail that they let me take the road test. Except I didn't, I still have no clue how the hell it happened, but I passed. It did give me enough play to sneak out from time to time and allow for some degree of a social life and freedom. Even then, I was still terrified to do much. I had to be calculating, thinking ahead to how to avoid being busted and getting home on time. Honestly, the only times I did stupid shit behind the wheel were to beat curfew.

The program had already been installed by that point. I possessed the anxiety-driven inability to go "all-in" on almost anything, perennially stuck in low gear. This gear complements a lack of self-confidence quite well. Slowly I am grasping it really is all about continuing to show up. Just keep showing the hell up, it really is most of the battle.

How could this be made tangible? Physically, it can start with learning healthy eating habits, setting aside enough time for adequate rest, and a commitment to exercise. Better physical shape should lead to more well-being, and that alone will work wonders on mental and emotional health.

As doors slowly open for me that I never envisioned, I keep reminding myself that I am worthy of everything I continue to be blessed with. The inability to feel deserving is at the core of my commitment issues, it can be incredibly difficult to accept love and abundance.

Amazing souls aligning with where I seek to be are continuing to enter my life. There are more people in tune than I ever realized. Truly it is humbling yet freeing to know that I'm not just some freak alone in the world. Mind-blowing opportunities just seem to keep appearing, which in turn leads to creating more ideas and possibilities. It's amazing what happens when you turn down the bullshit knob in your life. What is even crazier is I don't think I'm close to scratching the surface yet. Yeah, I know I am stuck dealing with some of the same bullshit, but the clock is ticking on that. Holy hell, so much has changed for the better in the last year. I NEVER in a million years saw myself headed down this path. Do I know where it leads ultimately? No, I never thought I would be blogging or posting videos on YouTube. If you told me a year ago I would spend a weekend at Kripalu I would've pointed at you and straight-up laughed with that heavy, loud, "I can't stop even though I'm not getting any oxygen" kind of laugh. I can't wait to see what else comes if I continue to just stay in that damn room.

Scene 9:
Winning

I really enjoy sports so I'm going to go down that road for a little bit. I promise the point isn't all sports related, you didn't buy a low-key sports book. Badass analogies are hard to pass up, so roll with me here, okay?

The Houston Astros just won a terrific World Series (I guess I wrote this entry in October 2017), the first championship in the team's history. I loved seeing the pure joy and elation that Houston fans were expressing. There's nothing quite like your first time and few better feelings than a community-wide group bonding experience, even if you are unsure if a baseball is puffed or stuffed. Everyone has that extra gleam in their eye and a spring in their step, an infectious feeling of pride that a championship brings out of us.

I've been blessed to experience this quite a few times in the last 15 years or so, being from Massachusetts. I have gotten to witness and enjoy quite a few runs to championships from the local professional sports teams. Those of you that hate the Boston teams and don't want to hear about this shit, you'll have to suck it up while I take a second to elaborate on the feeling of "HOLY SHIT DID THAT JUST HAPPEN?!?!?!" and the welling up of pride and emotion. I'm not talking about where they set their city on fire, I'll never ever understand that. Feeling that shock, followed by immense jubilation and local pride (forget that usually no one playing on the team is from there, that is irrelevant to my point). Sharing that experience with family and friends, parents with their children. Remembering those you wish could witness this moment. Memories that you have around this team flooding back to you. It just...I do hope that everyone gets to have that kind of an experience in their lives because there is nothing quite like it.

All that emotional release is from a great moment, but it's still something (unless we played for the team) that we have zero control over, and that ultimately has zero effect on our day to day lives. We still must go to our shitty jobs the next day, sit in the same shitty traffic as we commute to said jobs, and stress out over the same shitty bills we barely make enough to cover each month. Our responsibilities don't change, we simply can't blow off our parenting obligations or suddenly stop obeying laws because "YAY TEAM!"

Now let's ponder yet another idea. What if we could control having that feeling. Not because of the sports of course, but in our own everyday lives. What would it be like to have that joy because...US? Because we wake up in our souls, interacting, loving, living every moment through our souls? How fricking AMAZING would that be? Imagine all the incredible stuff that would go down on this planet if that were to happen.

Go ahead, take a minute. Close your eyes and visualize it. Take in everything you see, all that you can sense. Observe and embrace any emotions that come through. Just let go and immerse yourself in all of it. Your cheeky monkey mind may try to tell you that this is ridiculous. Let the monkey make its noise, that's okay, but keep it in the background. Just let the visual roll on. Admit it, you're loving this experience right now, aren't you? Your heart likely just skipped a couple of beats and you started getting those warm fuzzies inside, maybe even some chills or "butterflies"? Possibly feeling as though someone in the next room just chopped up some fresh onions?

When you've finally gone there and come back, I'll be here waiting with some homework. Yeah, I know, but you'll thank me later.

Please write down every detail that you remember about the experience. Every sight and sound in explicit detail. Every feeling that it drew up for you, and what it was that triggered those feelings. Be as thorough as you can possibly remember. Once that is complete, there is a second step: read through everything you wrote and find one thing that you can do RIGHT NOW to put you closer to living that experience. Even the smallest step is still an important one. Go ahead and find a little thing. Simple as opening a door for someone or taking a walk around the block. Turning off the TV or scrolling past that annoying jerk on Facebook. Telling someone you love them. Calling that friend that you've been meaning to for the past 6 months. Giving your kids an extra hug. The possibilities are endless, and you only need to come up with one thing.

Well, only one thing for today anyway. Tomorrow, go find another thing. Same with the next day, the one after that, and yes, the one after that. One thing every day. You will find that the itty-bitty leaps start to get just a little bigger and bigger as you start to see the results and how much better life is starting to feel. But just know that it doesn't always have to be some big, daunting, scary, expensive step all the time. The little "baby steps" are just as important. I promise you this.

When more and more of us keep taking these little steps, it will be like when you throw stones in a pond. When you start seeing those beautiful ripples emanating outward. Well, that ripple through life will be just as beautiful. How they say negativity spreads like a wildfire? This is true but the same can also be said for positivity. Love and joy can be spread just as fast if we want it to. Go for it, spread your little baby steps of joy all around you, and just watch it blossom. It'll be worth it, trust me.

Scene 10:
Snowflakes

Let's discuss "snowflakes" for a little bit, if you don't mind. "Snowflake" seems to be the go-to insult for everybody lately. Okay, there are certainly worse ones, as you can see from whatever social media timeline you choose to look at right now. But still though? People bitch constantly about others feeling "entitled" and expecting the world on a silver platter just because they want it. Millennials especially tend to get called out constantly over this. Look, there is a lot of that in our society, possibly stemming from "helicopter parenting", which leads to a lot of rude awakenings as this current generation starts making their way through adulthood. They're getting out into the "real world" and realizing that their employers don't give a crap about them, or anyone else. Which of course leads to "blah, blah, blah, bootstraps, blah, blah, blah…" Yeah, there is a lot more coddling than there was, and there are too damn many participation trophies handed out. But you know what? These kids know it's all unearned bullshit. That's why you see them under the bed or in the toy box. Additionally, they don't really know what they are capable of. They are taught that their worth comes through likes on Instagram and Snapchat followers, rather than the kind of human they are growing into. That sucks, they are doing the best they can and need more support from the real world than they are getting. Yup, their parents overdo it, never really letting them have opportunities to figure out their own shit, to fall hard and often. I am guessing some of it comes from the guilt both parents working their ass off outside of the house, and this is how they are taught to make up for it. They're not shitty parents. They were doing the best they could with what they knew.

Another factor is that these days most employers suck. Their only interest often is the bottom line, maximizing profit, minimizing cost, extracting every ounce of blood they can get from an employee. No fucks are given about developing their talents.

I also suspect that most people that bitch about them (remember, most complaining is a self-reflection whether one realizes it or not) are really pissed because they feel like they should have been treated better. I would agree with this deeper sentiment, it is overall a valid point.

Yes, everyone IS unique. Every single one of us could be special if allowed to channel their maximum potential. Every single one of us has their own "something" they can provide to make this gigantic blue marble a better place. We do, our children do, our parents do, and everyone out there bitching does. Yup, that's right. Now let it all out, go scream into a pillow or do whatever you have to do to collect your composure because I'm going to need you all to hear me out.

I am NOT saying that every child can or should be President, or a CEO, or a rock music icon, or a professional athlete. You get the idea. Not all callings are at this playing level, and they don't need to be. Maybe a calling isn't related to the working world. It could be based around a hobby or a cause. It may well be something you aren't ready to imagine because you are meant to create it and you simply haven't gotten there yet.

Consider this, so many things need to fall into place just right to create a human life. Yeah, the process is simple enough, but it involves two particular people out of however many billion finding and REALLY connecting with each other, even if only for a few minutes. With that it additionally involves whichever little swimmer out of however many million winning the "Spartan Spermy Sprint" and if the egg being in the proper condition to...please tell me you all know this shit by now! But you get the point, the odds of you being conceived exactly as you are so freaking ridiculous that someone has a better chance of getting struck by lightning twice while being kidnapped by aliens that just won the Powerball. Guess what? WE ARE ALL SPECIAL SNOWFLAKES! There you go everybody, Congratulations!

Solved that, so let's revisit the helicopter parenting. Another well-intentioned yet potentially catastrophic concept that doesn't prepare the young ones for what happens once they make their way out of the overprotective bubble. Yeah, of course you must protect the little ones a lot at the beginning. They will need everything at first and as they develop they will need less and less, gradually learning their independence appropriately and how to navigate stuff on their own. As they grow they need to be protected by the bullshit that youth life can throw at them. There are bullies and predators and other dangers out there so of course we all have to stay aware for their safety. As they mature, they do need to learn "street smarts" and how to protect themselves as needed. It's a gradual process like most things, with no true right answer and a lot of give and take through the process.

They also need to learn how to fail, to be given the opportunity to royally screw stuff up and fall flat on their faces. They need to learn to be able to get back up without Mommy and Daddy running to save them every time so that they have the bumps and bruises needed to make good life decisions. The current result is far too many adults incapable of handling their own shit. Think about it, how many of us have been in relationships where at least one involved party was unable to own and deal with failings, struggles, emotions, and tried to get needs met in inappropriate ways?

If your child is struggling with playing baseball or basketball or whatever, they need to learn how to get better. Let the coach do his or her thing with the child. Don't interfere, don't yell at the coach if your child doesn't start. Support the child while encouraging them to keep working, learning, and being a good teammate. Maybe they conclude that the sport isn't their thing. Respect their choice and let them try something else. Don't try to live your own dreams through your kids. Challenge them to find theirs and go at them with all the passion they can muster. Inspire and encourage them to get back up, learn, and work harder. Whether that gets them a trophy, real or participatory, next year is irrelevant, you're teaching the kids they must work and struggle and fight for their piece. This will be a valuable lesson for them as adults. They'll thank you later. It may not be until they are raising their own but trust me on this.

If your kid is failing math, they need to learn how to figure it out. They need you to encourage them to keep working at it, to keep up with their work. Help them as you can and support their teacher in the process. They DO NOT need you to harass the crap out of the teacher until they get sick of dealing with you and give your kid a passing grade just to get rid of you. Not your kid, you. Your child will know that grade is bullshit and will learn a bunch of unhealthy habits. Let them pass or fail on their own. If that means summer school and your beach vacation gets thrown out of whack, tough shit. They don't learn to work through it now, they're not going to know how when shit gets harder later.

One of the biggest gifts you can give your children is the opportunity to royally fuck something up, and then fix the situation on their own. They HAVE TO learn how to fall and how to get back up. Of course, it sucks to watch; there is nothing worse than seeing the most important soul in your life, that you love more than anything, be heartbroken after something doesn't work out. I understand that. But they need to be able to know how to feel these emotions, figure out how to work through them, realize that the world didn't end because they failed, get back up and eventually get it. What may be a rough ride now will serve them so much as they get out into the real world. They will know how to deal with the shit sandwiches that get thrown at them as adults, and be able to shine through despite them. Be support, space, love, and empathy of course, but let them grow and learn. If you do this then congratulations, you have done your part in adding one more emotionally strong human into the mix, and the world will be a better place for that.

Let them play and explore, create, build, write, dance, sing, whatever. Encourage their missions to discover who they are, what they want, what they believe, what their passions are. Even if they don't align with yours. ESPECIALLY if they don't align with yours. Embrace their uniqueness, their creativity, and their dreams. Let your kids figure out on their own who the hell they are and embrace them. All of them. Yeah, it can be a little kick to the ego when they wish to follow a different direction, and to live their lives differently. Didn't you do the same to some degree with your parents? They survived, as will you. Let them find the thing that makes their star shine, their soul sing. Let them find their own path to fulfillment and develop and share their unique gifts. Let them be snowflakes.

Scene 11:
"Man Up"

It's apparent when you meet me that I don't exactly fit the model of a "typical" Western male. Not that it should matter but let's face it, it often does. It has never quite felt comfortable fitting into that prototype. I find it difficult to relate, although these days I don't care anywhere near as much as I did in my twenties. Even then, it just felt like a shirt that didn't exactly fit. I mean, I like women and sports, and I can fix some stuff (just not cars though...build a cabinet, fix the dryer or the sink, rewire the living room? Sure. Bad things happen when I go near cars, though. It's been proven). My inability to relate to what society deems as "manly" has always been a battle. While I have always seen myself as being masculine, and have never at all questioned that, others have. I do get grilled at times on why I never shared stories of my "personal conquests", or why I'm not very open about when or who I am dating. I just never believed it was anyone's business other than the parties involved, plain and simple. Just because I don't discuss it does not mean that my masculine drives aren't present, my "alpha" is working quite well, thank you. I just do not need to give in to their every urge.

I feel like there's some kind of "balance" I'm trying to sustain, although I struggle with what that idea truly means. I was really only taught about both extremes of the "spectrum"; I was either "entitled" to go home with whoever I desired, or I was "scum" if I gave in to any of those said desires, or if I even asked. Confusing much? Yeah, I always knew neither extreme was a good thing (at least I grew up with THAT much sense), but I was totally on my own trying to figure out where the right balance was. The only thing I did know was that I was trying to seek it.

But while I figure out the whole balance thing, I at least have a better idea of what I desire in a female partner going forward, thanks to the litany of mistakes, errors, misunderstandings and flat out fuckups, which will all be laid out in my next book, *How to Fuck Things Up with Women Six Different Ways from Saturday*, due out on the 12th of Never. Seriously though, with all the learned dumbassery has come the gift of a better idea of what I am looking for in my next relationship, and the one after that, you get the idea. It may still feel like I am tiptoeing through an unfriendly village but at least the knowledge of what doesn't work for me helps.

But it is tough when, in a world loaded with "x" and "y", you're trying to find "z". But I also wonder, maybe we are ALL trying to find "z" but because we were only taught about "x" and "y" we don't know any better? Well, that would sure explain a whole lot of shit right there.

I think I am doing a decent job trying to explain from a solid masculine place, but it seems I continually get crickets and tumbleweeds as a response from my fellow men. God, it frustrates the shit out of me. When I speak of it, I try to come at things from a level where everyone is empowered, men and women, to assert their truths yet also be free with their emotions. Attempting to proceed in a way honoring both the divine masculine AND the divine feminine. I do not believe that we must choose one over the other, the hell with what society tells us. It feels like most men cannot relate to what I have to say. Occasionally you get the equivalent of a head nod, but that seems to be about it. I don't really know what that is supposed to mean. Do you really understand? Do you just not give a fuck? Do you think I am full of shit? Honestly if it's the latter I wish I would hear more about that, because I think it's worth having the conversation.

There are plenty of men that get it and live accordingly. I wish they would speak up a little bit more about it themselves. I guess they have their reasons, of course. Speaking up can be scary and having Grade A blowback firing at you can suck. Maybe there is simply a preference to live by example, or possibly some other reason that I don't know. I'll just continue to be a support to whoever needs that, and I promise to the best of my ability to listen intently, accept, ask for clarity, and answer without pontificating. Enough know-it-all blowhards exist, I don't need to add to it.

I accept that there is much work to do with these walls being so goddamn thick from centuries of a certain way of construction. It is what is, and we need to work with what we can and rebuild. Accept that this is a slow-paced project and that it'll need to be done with chisels instead of bulldozers.

It still seems many of us, especially men, are "broken" in different ways and that is going to be a very slow to fix project because of the way we are wired by our upbringings and by society. I am certainly no leader, and DEFINITELY not any sort of an expert or "guru" in these matters. Shit, I'm still trying to work through my own fucked up, tangled pile of wires myself. But I would like to be a useful tool in the box going forward, all shined up and raring to go. Until that time comes, I sit in service, working on improving.

Scene 12:
Mea Culpa (Mostly)

"Me too." It's all over our timelines. Impossible to miss or ignore, as it rightfully should be. I have always known that women are constantly subjected to a bunch of horrible, undeserved shit, including many of the women in my life. I know some of their stories, and it has broken me to see the pain in their eyes and words. A lot of that has come back up for me as I see every "me too" on my pages. I feel the fear, anger, sadness, and pain. I wish I can fix it all. I know this is impossible. However, that doesn't mean that I can't do my part to change things. I can learn from my mistakes. I can be a safe space for those in need. I can listen. I can be upfront and honest about my intentions and always communicate honestly, from my heart. I can accept rejection, not as an indictment of my lack of manhood but as a tool to learn and grow in my masculinity and my humanity. To move on. I can try to be an example to follow for the boys in my life, especially my nephew. And for the girls to know their choices need to be honored with no fear of consequences, especially my niece. I can speak up, and I can scream THIS IS NOT OKAY! NO MORE! NOT ON MY FUCKING WATCH! Whatever your experience, I ask of you reading, especially the men, to read the above and to vow the same: THIS IS NOT OKAY! NO MORE! NOT ON MY FUCKING WATCH! For our moms, sisters, daughters, and other loved ones, please.

I'm a puddle about writing this next part. There may be possible triggers involved so keep that in mind. I also understand some may think less of me after reading this. I have no control over that. After I wrote the above, I had mentioned that I knew I needed to whip up an additional piece with men in mind. A couple of very wise astute folks also mentioned this. I know it needs to be done.

At this point I have been staring at a blank page for days. I honestly don't know how I can go about it in the most authentic way, because I'm pretty fucked up. When it comes to dealing with the male side of things, I have a closet jam-packed with skeletons. Not all, but many do stem from my bad decisions. I cannot encourage others to work through their shit if I am not upfront with mine as best I can. This is not some bullshit attempt at collecting sympathy, that is not helpful to me or to anyone else. However, if I can let someone know that they are not alone, and if I can get people to talk about things in a more open manner without fear of being attacked for it, then it will be worth it. Fuck it, here goes....

First assault I remember was about 8 years old, by a much older, bigger girl that pinned me down and jammed her hand down my pants. Lot of pointing and laughing because of how small it was (no shit because I WAS FUCKING 8!!!). She came back around a second time with her large male friend that once had pulled a knife on me on the bus, he pinned me down (no knife that time I don't think) so she could show him. When I tried to tell someone later, no one believed me.

Multiple rejections and laughs at my expense continued to come as I grew. One girl that I had a crush on at age 13 pretended to show interest, only to lead me into a room where I got beat up. Sometimes it was a relief to just be told to fuck off. I learned to expect it. When I later matured and there was real interest, I pushed some wonderful girls away because I was wired to believe it was a trap.

As got older I never really was taught how to approach women. My "education" was just a barrage of conflicting messages that alternated between "why aren't you fucking their brains out, are you gay?" and "all men are scum, don't be scum". Yeah, I was pretty much on my own to figure it out and didn't necessarily want to bother, but life went on.

I was blackout drunk for my first sexual experience in college at 18. I remember none of it, only becoming aware it happened the next day at brunch when some young lady I didn't know came up to me and kissed me. That messed me up and I felt like I had done something horrible to her. We became friends after that for a while, but the guilt was always there.

The following summer, I met a wonderful young lady who I really clicked with when I went camping for a week with a friend. We took off for some alone time and neither one of us had a watch. She missed curfew by about 3 hours. They left the next day and any future attempts at contact were met with her father threatening bodily harm.

The rest of my 20s I was drunk more often than not, alternating between meaningless hookups and getting myself "friend-zoned" if I actually felt something. Friend-zoned. What a stupid fucking term. Here's the truth, I would have feelings for a woman and not have the balls to just come out and say it. I was always under the impression that if I was "wonderful enough" that a woman would see through my being ugly as fuck, then we would live happily ever after. Reality was they would either find someone else or figure out my bullshit and I would get a sudden cold shoulder. I always felt like an unlovable victim when all I was being was a douchebag. Granted I never realized this, I always thought I was a "nice guy" and not one of those "asshole" guys that they always fall for. They were at least upfront assholes. I was a spineless asshole who hid his true intentions, which I guess also made me a liar. It really shook my foundation when I reached this understanding.

Apparently when I grew some liquid courage I was more upfront with my intentions. My "conquests" occurred while shitfaced leading to many, many fuzzy details. I don't think I did anything really bad, but I cannot fully guarantee that this is the case. I think there was consent with everything and everyone, but I can't get past about 95% sure. I'll never know 100%, and I have to accept that and pray this was the case.

When reaching the end of my 20s, like with many other things, I pretty much gave up on any chance that I could be fixed enough to sustain any kind of healthy relationship. I met women that I had interest in but in my mind, what was the fucking point? Who is going to want this colossal disaster for a long-term partner?

Okay, some of my shit's now out there, enough with that. I imagine I am not the only one with a such a fucked-up background as that. Struggling to figure out how to act, what to do, and who to ask. That who to ask part? I never really had that in my life. Many of the men I knew hadn't got their shit together either because they were never taught themselves. I don't even know if there is an answer but it's something I try to study and read on as I'm figuring out all the other crap. I am working on trying to see myself as worthy of loving someone one day and being able to be loved.

But first comes first, continuing to learn to love myself in the face of my past. Accepting and learning from it, and understanding that my past is NOT me. Forgiving what has been done to me, but not forgetting the lessons about what unacceptable behavior is. Refraining from beating myself up for my own mistakes. Focusing on fostering connections from a place of kindness and love as much as possible. Tuning in and remaining open about what my heart feels in an honest way, regardless of the message that needs to be delivered. Accepting rejection with grace as simply another's perception.

Moving on with life when it's clear a relationship is no longer working out. Insisting on being treated in the same manner and willing to walk away otherwise.

I know that I'll make mistakes going forward. I am still and will always be a learning, growing being, interacting with others who are also learning and growing. I'm not sure what else I have left to say on this topic, I won't bullshit any answers just to fill space. Conversations do desperately need to continue, and I wish to be a positive force for that. Maybe I won't get every answer right on this, but I can vow to be a place of safe space, to listen, and to be of support for anyone needing any of these. It's not everything, but at least it's a start.

Scene 13:
Solitary Man

"No man is an island
Entire of itself
Every man is a piece of the continent,
A part of the main

If a clod be washed away by the sea,
Europe is the less,
As well as if a promotory were

Any man's death diminishes me,
Because I am involved in mankind.
And therefore never send to know for whom the
bell tolls;
It tolls for thee"
-John Doane

The preceding piece is in many ways a 400-year-old, terminologically outdated work. Is it really though? Isn't this so many of us, doing the whole "island" thing? Attempting to figure all this shit out on our own IS what it seems like we are all taught to do. That old "pull yourself up by the bootstraps" crap. Independence overkill is a prevalent masculine trait. I was taught that a man is to NEVER ask for help under almost any circumstances. Okay, occasionally the "male bonding" experiences, such as camping trips, watching football, or fixing a car. Yes, they're great connection moments but often only to a certain level, as much as is "allowed."

How many caveman "grunt, point, fart" jokes, or "asking for directions" jokes have we all laughed at? While we do joke, there is an issue on a much more serious level. We crack on the dude that tries to take the whole trunk full of groceries into the house at once, especially when half the bags rip, and calamity ensues (Been there, done that). However, don't we do that with our stresses and our emotions too? Don't our bags rip, often leading to far more damage than a shattered jar of pickles? Some serious fucking damage is inflicted to ourselves as well as others. When one has no idea how to deal with inner trauma and pain, it leads too often to our lashing out in anger, to others and especially to ourselves. There is a reason why the suicide completion rate is much, much higher in men.

Overall, many of us haven't truly learned how to effectively express what we feel internally. When it comes to bitching and moaning about politics or football or an idiot boss, we have that down solid. Communicating deeply about what's going on within is where we so often fall short. We bottle up our shit in way we think is tightly, but does it ever really work? Maybe for a while but then it eventually unravels. It may be something like tuning out your significant other in conversations or showing no interest in anything other than the news or the basketball game. Maybe it turns into punishing yourself inwardly through drinking, drugs, overeating, overworking, infidelity, or other issues. Sadly, it can release itself outwardly in the form of physical, sexual, or emotional violence.

It enrages me when I hear the horror stories that so many have lived because someone was incapable of appropriately expressing themselves. Between my years of work, and conversations with loved ones and acquaintances, I have heard too goddamn many. This has never diminished how much they trigger my feelings and emotions about this subject. I am glad that those feelings don't fade for me though. I would never want that to become something I got steeled to, because I feel a duty to keep trying to understand how and why this happens, so

I can help be a part of a solution. I feel a calling, I guess, to work toward finding the root of these problems. Committing to the work involved to seek out, identify, and repair the core pain that ignites these situations is the only way I can figure to get these bullshit cycles to stop.

I strongly believe in facing repercussions for criminally egregious acts, and assailants must serve the appropriate punishments. That said, I see another problem arise when they come out of prison just to repeat the same shit again and again. It's obviously not the entire solution. We need to do more than just punish the acts, we must figure out how this shit never happens in the first place.

What is needed is a full-blown paradigm shift, folks. We need to change what is meant by "acting manly", "handling our shit like a man", "taking it like a man", all mean. This model no longer works. Hell, did it ever REALLY work? Our men are broken, we're barely aware we have a problem, and we sure as hell have no solid plan to fix it.

This is NOT about "ending masculinity" as is sometimes heard. In fact, we NEED more "real men" and we need them right now. We need to understand what that really means, and we need to learn how we can get there. We need to learn to find our power without becoming oppressive, to find love while balancing our masculine urges, and to safely express our emotions, fears, wants, and needs. We have to learn to be okay with admitting we don't know what we don't know, asking for fucking help when we need it, and finding strength in what our hearts tell us we are. We need to ditch the masks and not concern ourselves with what we perceive society wants from us. We must practice true, authentic self-love and self-care.

I still admit that I have far more questions than answers in all of this. I don't believe anyone has all the answers, but that doesn't mean we can't keep learning. I know there are many other men who have that same desire to learn, and they may not know what to do with that. I am throwing my arms up and calling out with all of this in mind. We must begin to have these difficult conversations with ourselves, with those we love, and especially with other men. In the end it's up to all of us to change the paradigm. It is not going to magically happen for us.

We need to do this for the women we love, and to teach the children we love. There must be a day where they know that the bullshit is no longer acceptable. We need to for our fellow men, and especially our boys, because they need to see and experience better modeling of how to express, not repress. Most importantly, we need to do this for our own development. If we truly learn to come to peace with our own true being from a place of love and heart-centered compassion, then we will find that the masks will fall, the bullshit will stop, and everything will fall into place. We will begin to heal. It has been for far too long now and it's beyond time for this to happen. Let's crush this.

Scene 14:
Me vs Food

Ahhh...diet. How we fuel the amazing vessel that is the human body. The right amount of this, a little less of that, stay the hell away from this other thing....and then there is me. At times, I can be my own worst enemy. I do know that I really need to smarten up when it comes to my diet. I really have much room for improvement in this area.

It's quite the challenge. Everyone and their cousins have different ideas of what works and what doesn't, dependent upon what they may or may not be selling. I find more confusion with each article I read or video I watch. Whether or not I am actively trying to seek advice, I get plenty, usually from someone trying to sell some product. Thanks, but no thanks.

I would really like to do this on straight diet changes alone.

One thing I do know is that I need to strongly restrict if not eliminate sugar and grains, especially wheat, entirely. This is where the real struggle lies. Granted I don't eat a lot of sugary stuff, and haven't in quite a while, but then there's carbs...bread, pasta, more pasta, even more pasta. Yes, occasionally the sweets but I'll down a tray of mac and cheese if this is an option no matter how many cupcakes are next to it. I can't stop eating that stuff, even when I know I am full I just have to keep shoving that shit in my face.

I figured out that this is the stuff that REALLY gives me problems. I just bloat up like crazy, my intestines feel like they're under attack and it's just a miserable road. Very likely this the biggest reason why I am still beyond overweight. Yet even as I know this I can't help but blaze a trail to the refrigerator at all hours and attack. Just gorging myself with crap that is slowly killing me. Tasty crap, but still crap. What the fuck is the matter with me?

Yeah, I do enjoy other foods as well, yet I'll find myself not eating during the day. Sometimes I force myself to, but I usually don't bother. Then when I get to work at night I feel these urges to demolish anything edible that sits still in front of me. I'll feel almost dizzy, like my blood sugar is dropping in the car sometimes on the way in. My default answer is to stop at the convenience store and grab a slice of pizza, some chicken nuggets, or some other grease-filled concoction easy to wolf down as I drive. Good news, it clears out the lightheadedness issue in the moment. Now for the bad news, everything else.

Yeah, there is all kinds of regret, self-disparaging thoughts, beating myself up, all that fun shit. But it just serves as an engine for making even worse food decisions the rest of the night. There are donuts? GULP! An extra pizza? SNARF! Cookies? Brownies? CHOMP! Gee, considering how I feel about my job, you think I might be trying to fill some kind of a void there? Hmmm...Captain Obvious, what's your take on the situation?

Maybe I just need to attack myself preemptively before I get attacked by someone else? I think I may have just made a connection there. Yeah, amazing what you don't see when you choose not to, huh? Well, I guess I could start with accepting that I have a problem. It is what it is, I'm fat and I can't stop myself from comfort eating carbs. I need to learn to accept that and not only change it but to embrace those changes regardless of how much I really just don't want to.

Two things are for sure when it comes to diet. First, my attitude sucks. I know this, and I have to work through the "why." Second, I am leery to talk about it, especially on social media, because people seem to view my discussing it as an open invite to throw in their $0.02 about what I should do and how I should do it. Surprise, it's usually directly related to the product that they are selling. Now I have no problem with people doing their thing, dipping their toes into the entrepreneurial pool. I don't wish to deny anyone the opportunity to build on their confidence and their skill sets, and I truly do want to see people succeed in their endeavors. However, I'm not going to be your customer, or work in your pyramid or whatever that's called. Please spend your energy looking for someone who desires your product. I promise you that they are out there, I'm just not that guy.

Anyway, I know that I have to make some extreme changes to my diet. I am openly dreading this because it means saying goodbye to an old way of life. Sayonara to a significant part of my story. Adieu my love of all things pizza, pasta, and bread. Farewell to the drive thru and the perceived simplicity of buying shit that I can wolf down in the car because I didn't bother to properly prepare anything worthwhile before I felt ready to pass out.

Also, I fucking hate salads. I hate the idea of watching everyone else mow down these delicious pieces of heaven while I sit in the corner munching on carrot sticks. I hate the idea of not drinking beer. Not that I drink it very often these days, but when I do I fucking LOVE beer. I hate the idea of walking away from cookies, cupcakes, and ice cream shakes. Damn it!

So yeah, there is my attitude about food. Part of it. It gets worse. I also have this double-edged sword that I keep struggling with that makes it all worse. As I mentioned earlier, there are certain things that I cannot stop eating, that I will continue to devour until well past full. That I will raid the refrigerator to attack at 3 am. The vast majority of the binge targets are anything grain-based. Pasta will especially trigger the urges, but also bread and occasionally white rice. Generally, anything made of wheat I literally cannot stop crushing. It is fucking disgusting. I am ashamed to admit this, but I feel if I am asking others to be accountable that I should be doing the same.

Oh, and intestinal issues? After a lot of inconclusive testing, based on elimination I was able to figure out that one trigger is...you guessed it, wheat. By no means is it any sort of deadly allergy or anything like that, not yet. But my stomach will bloat out and my body will be in agony. I'll itch and just feel horrible. My brain feels like it is in a fog, and my moods go all over the place.

As you know this has led me to be quite a bit overweight, which I am pretty sensitive about. Not necessarily about being the butt of fat jokes, because I'll crack the first one to diffuse that. I do feel embarrassed about letting myself go like that. Getting yelled at by the doctor all the time. Almost failing to finish a 5k walk for my niece and scaring the crap out of my nephew when I almost fainted. Feeling winded by things that should be easy. Being prescribed statins for high cholesterol and blood pressure. Lacking in my confidence because I look like a human Weeble.

Jesus...seriously dude. How the fuck did I get here? It started when I was a kid, because of course it did. Like most kids, at dinner time we were not allowed to leave the table until we ate everything on our plates. Whether you liked it or not you had to eat all of it. Which used to lead to almost nightly hour-plus standoffs with the parents. Which they ended up winning eventually. Then I figured out if I actually did eat everything I could get a lot of praise! Being a human child, I liked praise. I aimed to please because it beat getting in trouble. When I cleaned my plate, my parents would be happy with me, and not be yelling at me. I learned to devour it all and return for seconds and sometimes thirds.

Even as a kid there were certain things that I loved to eat a little bit too much. Chicken nuggets. Spaghetti. Pizza. Pie. Mac and cheese.

Usually my mom would cook enough for about two meals worth for everybody, so there would be leftovers. Until I would regularly foil that strategy by demolishing them in the middle of the night. I would literally wake up at around 2 or 3 in the morning and just shove a crap-ton of food down my gullet. I knew it was bad, but I just couldn't stop regardless of how pissed off my mom would get at me.

It never dawned on anyone back then that this might be some kind of an emotional or other issue. They just thought I was being a little asshole. I failed to understand, I knew I couldn't stop but I had no clue why. Clearly it makes sense these days with what I now know. It wasn't like I really talked to anyone about what was bothering me, and definitely not my parents. I did everything in my power to hide as much as possible from them.

When you're a kid, your metabolism covers up a lot of ills. In your 20s a few weeks at the gym gets you back in line. Once you clear 30? Add to that a sedentary overnight job? You blow up like a balloon. Then you start to hate yourself, which you soothe by overeating, you gain even more weight, the cycle continues.

To try and take this on, I have decided to take a whack at this somewhat crazy elimination diet for 30 days. No grain. No sugar. No dairy. I'm going to see if this jump starts the metabolism a bit. Also, maybe it wipes out some of the other digestive issues.

There will also be some other changes. For example, coffee only in the morning, switching to teas for the rest of the day. Oh, and much more water. Lots and lots of high quality H2O. Now if this doesn't manage to kill me…

I need to try and curb some of this bullshit once and for all. I can't be looking to binge on crap for comfort or to bury my garbage. I should be out seeking connection and eliminating it altogether. People will help with that. Mac and cheese can't.

I am trying really hard to not see this as a punishment. Although I am internally freaking the fuck out about this, I'm trying to see as a mission to accomplish. I'm trying to use diet as a mechanism for self-release, to steer myself away from the dependence on food for comfort.

Continuing to carry all of this excess baggage causes me to feel as though I am in lack. I feel sloppy, awful, and sluggish as I am not getting the right fuel or the proper nutrients. I just generally feel lousy physically. It doesn't need to be this way.

When I was at Kripalu, the food served at the retreat center was so delicious, and so healthy. By Sunday morning, even as sleep deprived as I was I just felt so much better physically. Then there was Sunday afternoon, the trip home. I couldn't be on the road an hour without shooting myself in the foot apparently. For reasons unknown I felt compelled to hit a drive thru and load up on greasy shit. It likely had everything to do with all the stuff I was trying to process through from EOL and I wasn't ready for it, so I quickly dove into what I knew and immediately felt like a dumpster fire. I started to catch myself falling asleep on a mountain road and had to pull over for what ended up being a lengthy nap. Certainly not my proudest moment.

I got another recent reminder that food doesn't have to be created from shit to taste good. I was blessed to be invited over for dinner with a childhood friend. It was a wonderful night with her and her friends and family. She is a strict vegan and the spread was that evening. The meal was all so healthy and delicious. I felt good and had zero need to attack a drive thru on the way home.

Does this mean I intend to go vegan anytime soon? No, I need my meat and potatoes at times, even when I do eat healthy. Certainly, there is plenty of room for improvement. Where I tend to follow the heavy short-term comfort down the road to regret, I can work to choose the road to feeling good, eventually becoming "light". So, onto this diet I head. Now off to the grocery store with list and recipes in hand. Yes, an actual food shopping game plan. To have good shit around that I don't feel compelled to binge on at 3 AM.

Scene 15:
ASKING? What?!?!

I have always been taught that asking for ANYTHING is bad and "beneath" you. There are many times in the past where I have refused to ask for help financially even though it would have bailed me out of a situation. I knew my parents didn't have extra money, so that road was never an option. I couldn't swallow my pride and ask anyone else. Plus, the grief I would have to deal with if my parents found out wasn't worth it. So as far as others were concerned everything was awesome.

I became proficient at playing the "shell game" to stay financially afloat. You know, pull money that's supposed to go to A, use it to pay down B, figure out A later. I also had to make some hard choices as to what I would spend the little money I had on, this was especially true when my first business failed. Deciding whether to eat or to put gas in the car. Using burner phones when I could no longer afford my cell contract, because I knew I had to have something. Blowing off the car insurance so I could give SOMETHING to one of the kids on their birthday and crossing my fingers this isn't the month they catch on and cancel it. Anyway, these are things that if I swallowed my pride I could have gotten help with until I figured out my next idea but that didn't happen. When you are in constant panic over the basics, you are in zero space for productive creativity.

Decisions were generated from sheer desperation, in this case just giving up on everything and going back to work. It wasn't as simple as that, there were other factors involved. For the sake of this, let's keep it simple. It felt like the action that needed to happen in order to get back afloat. Which I generally did, but it came at a large cost. My health deteriorated big time. That first year back I went through a bunch of health crap. I started to have trouble with my neck and back. My cholesterol and blood pressure skyrocketed, to the point I was put on medication. I started having some issues with my digestion that no one could really diagnose, and I had to try and figure out on my own. I got so depressed that I started to consider suicide as a legitimate option. Honestly, the only reason I didn't just do it was because I couldn't put my niece and nephew through that kind of pain. I was certain no one else would even notice, convinced that I was just a colossal piece of shit in everyone else's eyes. But not the kids, they just saw me as their uncle and loved me as I was when it seemed no one else did.

So yeah, that was all a bundle of chuckles, just going from one circle of hell to another. It still feels really raw to talk about this, and my ego begs me to not discuss any of this out of fear that I will be thought of less. That same ego that begged me to not ask for help when I desperately needed it. So yeah, I'm going to say that this ego is not being terribly helpful.

Let's put the ego down for a second, give it a sandwich to keep it occupied. We shall just go into this a little deeper and ponder the idea of not asking for help. How many of us buy into the idea of being forced to fix our shit by ourselves? It's certainly what I was taught, and it is mostly well-intentioned advice. But is that ever REALLY the case? Think about it, even when we think we do it alone we can't. We are not designed to operate solely outside of any community. Why do some of us buy into this bullshit when it doesn't ever work that way? Does all of this put asking on a different light? It does for me somewhat, even though my ego keeps screaming like a monkey swinging through the jungle.

Working through my visions for what I want this whole project to become, I am realizing slowly that it is a must to step out of that comfort zone and just bare yourself out there. That it will take a LOT of support and a LOT of assistance for me to be successful with all of this. Which means I am going to have ask for help a lot and bust through that piece of shitty programming that I have embedded within me. Sales and marketing are simply about creative ways to ask for money, accepting that it is okay when in an upfront, heart-centered way. Plenty won't align and will never be interested in what you have to offer, but there is ALWAYS a potential audience. I need to be willing to step up and offer it in the right way. Just keep putting myself out there and I will find my base. Just like the quote in Field of Dreams: "If you build it, they will come."

One more thing to share, it may sound crazy but around the time I really started doing my work post-Kripalu, this voice at one point spoke to me, clear as a bell: "The money will be there. For all of it. Don't worry about it." OK! I'm working on that.

Scene 16:
Re-assimilation

I believe I am ready to bring people back into my life. I'm not the same person I was before I started this journey, and I don't know who exactly I am in the process of becoming, so I don't know how this may play out. I hope that it allows me to be of clearer mind, and to understand people a little bit better than I did. On the flip side, I also strive to do a better job staying clear of all the negative bullshit that inevitably comes from it. I would like to be better at challenging others' crap as I move along, or creating a jolt for others to figure out their own shit? I do realize that I can only control myself and that I can't force change, nor would I want to. I certainly would not mind if I could guide or nudge someone in that direction. For today though, all I can really do is just live in the moment and speak from the heart as much as possible.

Time to really work on the defensive instincts as well. There are certain situations where honestly, I can get to a place and feel myself strapping on the emotional armor and gathering my weapons of choice. I know that armor turns me into kind of an asshole. I strongly dislike the person I can become in these situations, but instinctively it's how I can be ready for the muck that awaits. When I walk in the door the old fight-or-flight mechanism kicks in. The defense shields are set to full, and that can turn me into a moody, abrasive prick.

Here's the thing, in my mind, I have NEVER, EVER initiated anything. I have convinced myself it has always been a return volley. Know there are always at least three versions of a story: yours, the other person's, and what actually happened. This doesn't mean someone is necessarily lying, they believe their recollections are what occurred. However, our minds recall events in a way that fits within our safety zones. Certain points will be altered in the memory banks in order to protect ourselves, which isn't very helpful to a situation if you're looking to diffuse it.

Some circumstances can seem so toxic that a negative mindset feels mandatory to navigate through those stormy waters. Does it really though? Can it hurt to try things in an attempt to change the dynamics? What's the worst that can happen, it fails miserably, and you are in the same place you started? Give it a whirl if you're stuck there anyway but do so in small bits at a time. Change can be quite overwhelming to many, especially if you attempt to flip something big right away. Even little incremental changes can get shot down at times though. I've experienced plenty of this. The challenge there is to not let that beat you down or suck you into a toxic black hole. Be warned, also from experience, that if you're forced to stick around, it is much easier said than done. I've let it defeat me enough times to know.

If that's the case, then it's time to figure out how to cut your losses and begin to remove yourself from that environment. It is easy to say and much more difficult to accomplish, especially when in toxic employment, it's very hard to walk out if you are living paycheck to paycheck. Jobs that pay well and improve your well-being can be a challenge to find depending on your skill sets, which are always larger than you realize. It may be for the best interest of your own personal growth to relocate to another, significantly less toxic environment, even if it's just a temporary landing. Of course, to leap and do your own thing is always an option, but it takes some serious balls and it is a high stakes gamble that you must be fully ready to play out, including all the highs lows. If you're not in the right space it may be a ride you are not quite ready to take. Know that it does take a ton of hard and heavy inner work to get where you'll be able to ride the ocean wave you're going to land in.

Two questions will gnaw at you as you prepare the great escape:
1. What are the other important people in your life going to think?
2. Where the hell am I going to get money from?

These are very important questions, and to encourage people to blow them off would be very foolish. Many will question whether you have lost your mind. Most will do so out of concern and well-meaning. Let them be heard, but don't let them deter you from the mission. Remember that they see things from their own eyes and may just not understand what you are up to. That is perfectly okay. Give them their space, love them, and the ones that are truly in your corner will still be there. There are others who ultimately will not be. Some will be upfront about it, while others will either express it subtly or hold off until you are not present to speak their peace. This is important knowledge to have, so while you will need to walk away from them in the end, be grateful to know the truth. That can sting but it truly is a gift to know who has your back, so try to see it that way.

Regarding the money question, just have faith in what it is that you offer. Try not to see things in terms of dollars or numbers, as this will limit the crap out of your creativity. Just trust your shit. You have creative stuff coming out of all your orifices, we all do. It's a matter of letting go of the confining bullshit your "monkey mind" tosses all around. Keep locking in on your creative soul, it will not only guide you to what you offer the world, but also to finding those who are yearning to consume what you create. They are out there, even if it doesn't feel that way in the moment. I promise you that. The universe (or source, God, Alfred, whatever you call it) will always provide in abundance if you lock into your creative tool chest and keep on working out if it. The money, the numbers? They will come, trust in that. Let the worries go and do not surrender to them, no matter how scary they may make things look. I cannot say this enough, trust your shit. Dive in and ride the waves. Keep rolling.

Scene 17:
Haters Hate, Pleasers Please

We are all different and unique, in case I've forgotten to mention that. Mostly, that is a beautiful thing, with people finding their own voices and seeking their own places in this world. Cold hard reality is that you are just not going to like everybody, and not everybody is going to like you. That is just how it is, your truth is not going to align with everyone else's. This of course doesn't mean that you quit, it is NEVER worth surrendering that to appease anyone. Unless you are seeking relationships that are built on shoddy foundations destined to crash and burn, and what would be the point in the first place?

I come with this as a recovering "people pleaser" myself. Shit, most of my life has been about pleasing others. It's what led to my going back home when I left college rather than accepting a very interesting out of state job offer. It was why I even went to college in the first place. Now don't get me wrong, I had the time of my life there but the only reason I went was to satisfy others' expectations.

Part of my anxiety and depression issues, certainly as an adult, stemmed from knowing I cheated myself to make others happy. Trying to fit into a round hole as a square peg seemed to be the solution for making myself more acceptable in their eyes. What I wasn't getting is many of those from whom you give yourself up for affection, attention, or whatever end up kicking you to the curb anyway. Compromising yourself with squat to show for it is a painful experience shared by many. Most reading this have been there, done that and get how much that sucks. You will get a much-needed education as you learn who is really in your corner, and who is not, and these stinging revelations will shake your foundation. Figuring that out has been certainly quite the awakening on my end. For how much it can and does suck, it is better knowing the truth. This important information is only helpful as you get past it and roll back on. It is a blessing knowing who you can and cannot trust, and you can navigate free and clear moving forward.

It's your job to grow into who you need to become. It is NOT your responsibility to satisfy anyone else. It is true that anyone's perception of you has everything to do with who they are and nothing that you ever had any control over anyway. Likewise, your perception of them is strictly a reflection of who YOU are and has nothing to do with them. Even as you learn and grow, you are still human. You still possess your beliefs, values, experiences, and emotions, and you will continue to see life through those filters. It isn't about good or bad, right or wrong, just being human and the frailties that can come with that. Remember, in everyone's individual world they are the good guy. That's just how it works.

As you continue to find and grow your voice, you will find that some love it and others won't so much. You'll inevitably trigger some people and you will have zero control over their reactions, because once something leaves you, whether through writing, art, video, or anything else, it comes down to the message perceived, not the intent of the sender. It is what it is, and all you can do is accept it.

I was listening to a Wayne Dyer audio (The Erroneous Zones) recently. The good doctor made a great point about this. It was an older recording and he used the 1972 U.S. Presidential Election as an example. Richard Nixon obviously won in a landslide, taking 49 states. But when you collected all the votes together, he only garnered about 53% of them. Think about that, just a little more than half of the voting public liking you constitutes a landslide. Almost half didn't want him, and it was still considered a landslide victory. That isn't a whole hell of a lot.

Some better news, we're not politicians so we don't even need to worry about whether or not large amounts of people like us. It doesn't matter if most don't or most are indifferent. All we need to do is find OUR people, OUR audience. Those that NEED to hear our voice.

Remember that concept as you fight off that instinct to "people please". It's not worth ever giving up your value or your truth to placate the wants of others, especially when their support of you is about as strong as a wet paper bag. Even if you have only a few at first behind you, as you grow into your voice you will build an "army" that WILL have your back. The hell with the rest, let them be free to seek their own space and their own truth. Just keep finding yours. Think back to the video for "No Rain" by the underrated band Blind Melon. Remember that dancing girl in the bee suit who just kept looking and looking for her place to the point where she didn't think she would ever find it...until she did? That field at the end where there were all kinds of people dancing in bee costumes? Well, I promise your field is out there, so don't settle for being in a place that doesn't fit you. Keep looking, I swear that you will find it. The world is so wide open and there is a place for everyone to be seen and heard as they truly are. If you don't believe anything else that I have written about, please at least accept this. Trust me.

Scene 18:
The Creed of the Beacon

Once upon a time while attempting to bust out of a writer's block, I had this bright idea of creating a creed, basically a set of beliefs for how to proceed. Naturally I came up with a whole bunch of ideas.

1. We will seek from a place of love and not fear.

2. We will seek out and expect the best from all people, especially ourselves.

3. We are all connected to each other and the universe, but we also stand strong as individuals.

4. We cannot be of proper service to others if we have not cared for ourselves properly.

5. We are eternal learners, seeking to educate ourselves about our outer and inner worlds.

6. We will listen to and question ourselves as often as we do others.

7. We are all a work in progress: continually growing, evolving, and learning.

8. We will fail, and we will learn from our failures as much as from our successes.

9. We will seek to understand before we criticize. This does not mean that we do not call out the wrongs in the world. It means that we seek to understand why it is being done in the hopes of finding a solution.

10. Attacks are not an impression of us but the perception of us in the mind of the attacker. It is theirs, not yours.

11. With that in mind, when you call out someone's wrongs, it is also your perception of the other. Treat it appropriately. "I do not like your action because I felt________"

12. Accept that you cannot change others and they can only change themselves.

13. Blah blah blah blah blah blah blah blah blah blah blah blah blah blah blah blah.

14. Something that sounded like it came from Charlie Brown's parents.

I got to number 15, and I had a whole bunch more in my head. Then I went back to reread what was there and my first thought was, "What the hell is this shit? All of this? Really? I quit!" If that was MY reaction, and I wrote them, imagine how quickly this would turn off readers? So, back to the drawing board I went. I need something short and sweet but gets the point across. Then the Captain Obvious light popped on.

The Golden Rule!! Rainbows popped up everywhere and trumpets sounded from the heavens. Treat others as you would want others to treat you. Do unto others as you would have others do unto you.

Just about every religion has this, and it's not something with which one would need a religion to follow, pretty simple concept. That could work, right? Mostly, yes, but there was one little, important piece missing. So much of the idea of Beacon revolves around the belief that you must care for yourself before you can be of true service to others. It's probably something that I might want to incorporate as well.

Additionally, much of the hate, violence, and general nastiness we see in humanity comes from a need to lash out from inner pain and fear. That is a strong indicator, so it would seem, that the self is not completely healthy, and likely getting beat up pretty good. If one does not care for, or even hates their self, then "do unto others…" doesn't really mean a whole lot, does it? Talk about a loophole one can drive a tractor trailer through. That will need just a little tightening up.

Hold the presses, I think I have got it: "Treat yourself like the amazing gift you are, then treat others the same."

By golly, I think we have it. The Creed of the Beacon. Again, for those in the back: "Treat yourself like the amazing gift you are, then treat others the same."

Short, sweet, and to the point. Gets the message across. I think I am going to keep it. Now to find a place for those 37 or so other beliefs that were swimming around in my head......

Scene 19:
OK, Now What?

Well, I just spent a bunch of chapters going into certain areas of my house, some parts darker than others. I could have gone deeper into every one of them, but I felt like I had enough to say to at least start stirring up conversations and allowing a space for others to share their stories. If we don't have dialogue, brainstorming, sharing, any other give and take, then there was no point in my writing any of this. I feel like in time these topics can and will be discussed deeper and besides, does anybody REALLY want to read a book that can also double as a doorstop? Exactly. Other books may come in the future depending on what I may or may not be called to do. Maybe one of you reading feels called to build off something here and take it to the next step. That would be awesome. Even if the name of your book was "Rich Levesque is Full of Shit", I'd be down with this. I would even buy 20. Hey, attention is attention, right?

Anyway, I can generalize what my mission is for writing about all of this, and whatever comes up for me next that I cannot quite see yet, into three general points:

1. We are fed a ginormous pile of shit which generally has us all fucked up.
2. Now that we realize that, it is time for us to figure out how to clean up said ginormous shit pile.
3. Once the shit is cleaned up, we are left with who we truly are and who we are supposed to be.

The pile of shit builds up from almost the second we are shot out of the womb and into the world. We are born blank slates and we learn based on those around us, how to earn their approval and avoid punishment. Sort of like puppies, except with two feet and no fur. We get whacked with the newspaper when our behavior is deemed "bad" and our bellies get rubbed when we do "good". Primarily those we seek favor from are our parents, but not exclusively. In some ways this is unavoidable because we do have to learn to coexist within the reasonable parameters laid out by society. Most of the time we are molded by people who love us and really do the best they can despite their own faulty wiring getting in their way. Along the way, that faulty wiring usually gets passed along.

We learn a lot of garbage. We are only allowed to explore certain areas and levels. We settle for what is "expected" rather than what piques our curiosity and passion. We learn to bury our feelings way the hell inside of ourselves. Be a good boy or girl, take heed and follow to keep getting tasty treats and avoiding the newspaper. This happens to all of us to some degree, and many of us did end spent our formative years in some toxic shit.

Then we all go to school, where we further conform. We learn to stand in line, crank out our book reports, finish our math problems, pass our state-mandated tests. Teachers are restrained from exhibiting their true amazingness because they are ordered to stay within the standards, never to veer far off that path because people may question or complain, and administrators are more concerned with protecting their well-paid positions and their status than in defending their gifted staff, no different than most leadership. Back in the classrooms, kids become divided into their perceived ability levels, whatever that means. These often lead to certain "hierarchies" becoming entrenched among the student body, determining who are the "cool kids", who gets bullied, all that horseshit. All the young sheep are sorted and eventually farmed out to their fates. Some head to life as an hourly drone for the next 40 or so years, unless the company employing them decides that they would rather make more profit and shitcan them first. Others are shipped off to college where they may get better paying jobs but are saddled with so much debt that it doesn't really matter, chasing a middling career they were told is their best path to success.

Next in the game is to find a mate, often convincing ourselves we have found true love when we have simply settled. The following step is to buy a house, complete with additional debt and white picket fence. Now with the house come the 2.7 children, which have to be raised perfectly in the judging eyes of our parents, the neighbors, and members of the local PTA. They must have all of their free time tied up in activities that do not include being kids and receiving participation trophies that teach them jack shit. Oh, and they're slowly going down the same conveyor belts we did. Meanwhile, we get promoted up to a middle management position directly connected to how adept we are at ass-kissing and back-stabbing. Eventually, we put in our years and we retire, if we have managed to save enough money to do so without losing it in a Ponzi scheme. Even then, we only get to enjoy a few years before health gradually fades. You know how the movie ends from there.

As we follow the acceptable path of life, we have a society telling us we suck unless we buy this car, or watch this show, or take these pills. All of these will make us more "acceptable" to society. We buy into fabricated beliefs designed to divide us to the point where we dehumanize each other, and then we wonder why nothing gets accomplished.

So yeah, that's us in a nutshell. Now that we know that we can do something about it, how do we escape these chains and stop settling for this bullshit that is gradually killing us? I've talked of a couple things in here to work through some of these processes, but that really isn't my primary strength. There are many wonderful souls with incredible means of being able to help you out. Some of us have some seriously hardcore shit to work through and may need to go the therapy route. I did for a time and after burning through several therapists that I tuned out or otherwise just failed to connect with, I was able to connect with a tremendous one who gave me some amazing tools for working through my crap both now and in the future. That was where the bulk of the monkey clearing exercises from earlier came from.

Many of us may not need therapy, but there are still supports available. There are many different kinds of services available to everyone, you just have to look around and do research to figure out what works best for you. There will be that one voice or several voices that just connect with you. Look, keep looking until you find the one that clicks with you. Whether it's through life coaching, Reiki healing, EFT tapping, just freaking find it (If you don't know what any of these are, use Google). Get those goddamn boulders blown out, get that shit cleared up. Just fucking do it.

Then shit starts to get fun. You got all your crap cleared out and you're left with who you are. Now it's time to go play. Go find the thing that sings to you. Go find the place that has been calling you, the craft, the career. Find that heart space and listen to what it tells you. Then go and do it. Don't worry about what anyone else's opinion is. If they are truly with you, they won't go anywhere. Maybe you'll inspire them as you do the thing! Go enjoy the shit out of the rest of your life without answering to anyone else but yourself. Show everyone that they can do the same, and that life doesn't have to be lived in the mundane, the routine, the miserable, the bullshit.

GO BE A BEACON!!!!!!!!!!

Scene 20:
Thanks for Not Burning My Book!

Hopefully you, the reader, got some worth out of this book. There was a lot of thought, passion, emotions, sweat, tears, popsicle headaches, doubt, glory, and most of all, love put into this. The hope is that you didn't agree with everything I wrote. I would like to think that there were parts where you screamed "Hell yeah!!!", but I also suspect there were areas where the thought process went more along the lines of "Wait, what?", "I'm not comfortable with this", or maybe even "This is bullshit!" Cool!

I'm not looking to attract blind followers to this mission. I want to stimulate thought and provoke real and deep conversations. Not the debate crap you see on TV and in social media, but real, vulnerable expressions about our beliefs, values, and passions. I want you to really think about whether you are living in alignment, or if you are simply settling into society's crappy expectations. From there, figuring out how to navigate the gap in between the two.

I challenge you to share this book with others in your life and to invite these conversations. I think you'll find that the hardest thing to do is start them. Once you're past that point of no return, you'll work past the crap and on into the heart. When speaking from there the conversation suddenly becomes very easy. You may be surprised by what comes flowing out, so be prepared. The heart can only speak truth. When it comes, follow it always. It knows what is right for you and where you should be. It is connected to the universal source (God, the universe, nature, Elvis Presley, it's all good). Trust it hard, even if it feels bizarre. Let's keep thinking, seeking, wondering, and talking.

I do thank you kindly for sacrificing a few bucks and spending several hours with me. We all must make choices with our time and money, and I am honored you found my book worthy of both. If you did enjoy it, please feel free to give it a kind review and spread the word so that others may be able to find these messages. I wish you peace, love, and happiness in your individual journeys.

The Curtain Call: Acknowledgements

- **Sandra Levesque** You gave me the world, literally. I feel you around me during all of this, I really do hope that I am making you proud. I love you and miss you so much Mom, every day.

- **Richard Levesque, Sr.** Among many things you taught me is that it was okay to write the way you talk. There is a lot more of you in me than you give yourself credit for Dad, love you.

- **Benjamin Levesque** and **Alicia Levesque** for being the best brother and sister-in-law a dude could ask for, for always supporting me even when you were sure I was nuts. I love you guys.

- **Hannah Levesque** and **Andrew Levesque,** you two angels are simply my world. You are the reason I kept going and hold on to hope. May you two always stay true to yourselves and grab everything you want from this world. I love you both so much.

- **Scott Simoes** and **Stephen Vandenburgh** my boys since pretty much the dawn of time. For sticking around through phases, moods, and all the different crazy stuff the years have brought.

- **Lydia St Laurent** you saw my worth when I couldn't and I can never thank you enough for that. Undyingly loyal yet never putting up with my crap; you are as true a friend as anyone can be blessed to have.

•   **Melissa Jantz** for screwing my head back on straight and convincing me to process what I couldn't speak through writing. I learned how to do both in the process.

•   **Kyle Cease** for challenging me to "write the damn book" and telling me that I had a message that the world needed to hear. Well, I wrote the damn book. Thank you for that and being "that guy" I could relate to when I couldn't "hear" many others.

•   **Richard Stevens** for creating my first web page and insisting that my work was worthy of one when I was still processing the idea that I could write pieces legibly and in a way that resonated with people.

•   **Jodi Evans** for seeing the guy struggling to make his first video and pushing him to finally see how powerful his voice could be. Thank you for inspiring me.

- **Dori Gilbert** for our powerful "author chats" that helped screw my head on straight.

- **Jessie Wright** for being so supportive and not letting me stray, keeping me in line in a very loving way.

- **Trish Fellner** for her kind encouragement at impeccably perfect times. Some people just "know" when somebody needs a pick-me-up. She always does.

- The "Group of Eight", who got thrown together by a random video chat and by magic became family: **Ashley Maden, Christy Lodato, Cliff Cannon,**

James Paniagua, Kelly Larsen, Lisa Worthy, Nanette Duford.

There are so, so many more. So many who have been so supportive on my Facebook and Instagram pages, in my Beacon House group, in the Innie Sanctum and Blissfully Introverted, And in the EOL Communities, especially the Joy Love Bus. You all know who you are, and you are all so amazing. Social media gets an often-deserved bad wrap because of how it can be used, but there is also so, so much awesome and wonderful that comes from there as well. These people are proof positive of this.

One more acknowledgement: **Earth**. They say that this place is a giant wasteland filled with negativity, conflict, suffering. And in a lot of ways it is. But there is also a lot of good out there. More good than bad. The good stuff just never makes the

6 o'clock news. But it's there. We just have to look for it.

And now, time to score some tacos. Toodles.

www.ingramcontent.com/pod-product-compliance
Lightning Source LLC
Chambersburg PA
CBHW061341250726
48657CB00004B/1272